An Ultimate Truth

How to get **out** of dysfunction instead of **in** to recovery

Geoffrey Hamilton

PUBLISHING

A division of
Northwoods
Consulting

AN ULTIMATE TRUTH

How to get <u>out</u> of dysfunction instead of <u>in</u> to recovery

by

Geoffrey Hamilton

HIGH GROUND PUBLISHING

Published by:
High Ground Publishing
a division of Northwoods Consulting
6107 SW Murray Blvd. Suite # 351
Beaverton, Oregon 97008-4467

All rights reserved. Except as permitted under the United States Copyright Act of 1976, the reproduction, distribution or transmission of any part of this book, in any form, by any means whatsoever, electronic or mechanical, including photocopying, recording or any information storage and retrieval system, must first receive written permission from the author. Reviewers have authorization and permission to quote brief excerpts.

Copyright © 1997 by Geoffrey Hamilton

First Edition

ISBN 0-9654915-7-9
Library of Congress Catalog Card Number: 96-78426
Library of Congress Cataloging-in-Publication Data available upon request
Printed and manufactured in the United States of America
1   3   5   7   9   10   8   6   4   2

Dedication

I dedicate this book, first and foremost, to a concept: the idea that we humans can walk the course of heroes. I salute the heroic in those who have the courage to choose to live their lives on the basis of reason and responsibility. I want to offer my deepest respect to those who have chosen to celebrate the magnificence of the human spirit through their every belief, choice, and emotion. To all of you, I proudly say, "Well done!"

To those of my many clients who have chosen to walk the steep path and who have taken the 'high ground,' by fighting for it, I say "Thank you for allowing me the privilege of accompanying you and guiding you on your heroic journey."

To the following individuals who have especially inspired me by showing me exactly what a hero's journey looks like, and to whom this book represents a tribute:

Deborah L. Trevvett, my wife.

Vaschahar Havar, DPS. Ph.D. (deceased), my friend.

Ayn Rand (deceased), my inspiration.

Foreword

It is refreshing to read this work. With incisiveness, Geoffrey Hamilton dissects the causes of psychologic dysfunction. His discussions are quite lucid, exhibiting a clarity that greatly eases the task of reading about the complicated subject of mental processes.

This book is good news for those afflicted with mental pain and suffering. There is a way out. Hamilton has delineated a clear-cut, consistent means by which individuals can work their way free of psychologic dysfunction. It does take work; it is not easy. But, it does hold a real promise for relief from mental stress.

Some might question Hamilton's view of life as a task, a job, albeit a job of reaching fulfillment through the resolution of problems so that they can move in the direction of development and celebration. However, the emphasis upon life as a task is particularly relevant since the book is directed toward those who would reach much greater fulfillment in their lives if they had the ability to overcome their problems and could consistently work toward relief of those problems.

Also, some might question Hamilton's stress on persistent vigilance. This continuous vigilance could seem to negate the possibility for that happiness which is associated with the free openness of spontaneity. Nevertheless, vigilance is not necessarily inconsistent with spontaneity. If you enjoy rope-skipping, you still maintain balance while jumping.

Likewise, the emphasis on the self — self-examination and self-protection — does not rule out fulfillment through experience that is shared with someone else. In fact, when there is a resolution of psychologic dysfunction by means of the procedures discussed in this book, a much greater possibility presents itself for experiencing the joy of sharing all of life's events and pleasures.

Foreword

Hamilton goes into sharp, clear detail in his analysis of distress and guilt. He also includes an excellent section on the roles played in mental life by concern with "perfection" and the expectations of others.

This book presents an enlightening discussion of the dynamics of repressed emotions, including repressed anger. There is also an excellent delineation of the mental processes involved in codependency.

Hamilton's particular, dominant theme is the uncovering of core beliefs. These set the stage for much of the way life is lived. And, they are usually hidden from view. Many people do not realize what their core beliefs are.

Often these core beliefs are quite destructive impediments to happiness. Their harmful effects usually emanate from painful childhood experiences. Core beliefs permeate psychologic life and, most of the time, remain as unknown components. In Hamilton's analysis, unrealistic core beliefs are the primary source of mental dysfunction.

Hamilton presents an excellent procedure for uncovering core beliefs. He gives readers a clear-cut description of the means by which they can discover those basic beliefs which influence their entire lives. Also, he shows how to mitigate the effects of these beliefs. His method describes how a reader can be enabled to grow beyond those beliefs which have stifled his or her well-being. He shows that, with significant effort, a person can lift himself or herself from a life of anxiety and dysfunction to a life of psychologic health. The value of this book makes it well worth both reading and utilizing.

Ernest Lane M.D.

An Ultimate Truth

Acknowledgments

I must gratefully acknowledge the input of a great many people. They have all supported my objective, to complete this book, in many different ways.

My deepest gratitude, for the most profound support imaginable, can only go to my wife, Deborah. I hope that one day you may get to read *her* story. In my opinion, she embodies 'the hero's journey,' to the 'high ground' that she fought for and earned, more than any human I have ever had the joy to know.

To all my clients over the years, whom I cannot name, thank you from the bottom of my heart for letting me walk with you and learn from you.

My great thanks to Ernest Lane M.D. who not only edited this work but, in addition, voluntarily took the time away from writing his own book to write the foreword to mine.

Antony Bakke, Ph.D. not only helped to edit the manuscript but shared his valuable insights as a scientist, researcher and volunteer counselor.

To Anita Bobinet, Ph.D. I give my thanks for editing the manuscript and for bringing her expertise in the field of Speech-Language Pathology to bear where needed.

Dean Bobinet, RPh., M.S. gets a big dose of my gratitude for helping to edit the manuscript and finding the time to do so. I especially appreciate his point of view.

D. David Bourland Jr., of whom I will say more shortly, gets the blame for giving me *such* a headache when I started to write in E-Prime, which he created.

I wrote this book entirely in E-Prime. E-Prime defines the English language without any form of the verb 'to be.' To write in E-Prime requires much more than word substitution. It requires a

Acknowledgments

different, more precise way of thinking. It also requires some aspirins in the beginning.

If you want a real challenge sometime, try to rewrite something that already exists without using 'be, is, am, was, are, been, were or being.'

As a simple example, you cannot say that John 'is' a farmer because John's identity encompasses much more than just farming. John also functions as a father, son, husband, deacon of the church, cousin, uncle, mechanic, etc. The label 'farmer' only represents *one* of John's many aspects.

You could say that John farms; John owns 100 acres; John raises chickens; John inherited his farm from his father; John breeds prize winning horses etc. Any of these statements bring precision and accuracy to the characterization of John's identity.

"E-Prime forces one relentlessly to confront sloppiness, laziness, fuzziness, blandness, imprecision, simplistic generalization and a half dozen other all to frequent characteristics of casual prose."

Cullen Murphy, Managing Editor, The Atlantic Monthly

I want to acknowledge my gratitude to D. David Bourland Jr. who created E-Prime in 1965. I want to thank him for creating E-Prime in the first place and for personally reviewing my manuscript in the second place. I would like to share an excerpt from his review with you.

"From my viewpoint, a fundamental strength of Hamilton's work consists of his focus on the matter of evaluation. He presents a functional model of psychological processes which explains how early, perhaps inappropriate, beliefs can drop into our 'below conscious' mind and lead to various dysfunctions. He gives techniques for becoming conscious of our 'hidden drivers,' and replacing them with what some might call more mature, reasoned beliefs. He helps folks recognize that the responsibility for such revisions reside in themselves, not with some all-knowing therapist. In his summary about core beliefs, he gives this directive: "Value your life and live. Devalue it and die. You pick."

An Ultimate Truth

He discusses the formation of our early core beliefs, and what to do about changing those beliefs (if we subsequently feel it necessary).

In his comments concerning the genetic aspects of language, some will feel happy to note that Hamilton adopts a non-Chomskian attitude, without falling into the trap of Bloomfieldian behaviorism. Hamilton has some appropriately devastating comments on organized religions, including the steps necessary to organize one of your own, for power and profit.

His book seems extremely clearly written, in part due to his use of E-Prime."

D. David Bourland Jr., retired Associate Professor of Linguistics, creator of E-Prime, President of the Semantics Research Corporation, Vice President/Development of the International Society for General Semantics.

About The Author

Geoffrey Hamilton, born in 1940, maintains an active practice as a mental health researcher/educator, lecturer and management consultant.

He offers private training for individuals and groups concerning how to apply the principles and models of this text within various therapeutic environments. You can reach him in care of the publisher.

He encourages readers to let his publisher know which chapter, or chapters, in *this* book they would like to see expanded upon in his *next* book.

He also recommends that all readers of *An Ultimate Truth*, whether professional semanticists or 'just plain folks' like the rest of us, remember that *'An'* does not equal *'The.'*

About the Publisher

High Ground Publishing, a division of Northwoods Consulting, has as its mission the publication of previously unpublished works **that recognize, uplift and celebrate the heroic nature of human life from a rational, reasoned and objective point of view, free of mysticism and magic.**

Manuscripts that meet these requirements will receive a serious evaluation. Adult nonfiction preferred, fiction considered. No poetry or books for children.

Manuscripts must include SASE if the author wants it returned.

No agents, authors only.

Warning-Disclaimer

This book provides information on the topic of dysfunction with the understanding that the author and the publisher do not engage in rendering medical advice. If medical advice or any other professional expert services become necessary, you should consult with a competent professional.

Under no circumstances should the information in this book, or any other book, replace, or act as a substitute for, competent psychological or psychiatric medical advice from a licensed professional.

The publisher has made every effort to print this book completely and accurately. However, typographical errors and misstatements might conceivably occur. Therefore, this text should serve primarily as a guide and should not take on the status of the immutable, absolute, final, last word on the topic of dysfunction. Furthermore, this text contains information identified, by the author, as current up to the printing date.

This book has as its mission the education and edification of the reader. Anyone who reads this book agrees to hold the author and the publisher of this book free and harmless from any liability of any kind. The author and High Ground Publishing, a division of Northwoods Consulting, shall have neither liability nor any responsibility whatsoever to any person or entity with respect to any loss or damage caused, or alleged to have resulted from, directly or indirectly, the information contained in this book.

If you do not wish to accept full responsibility for the above, you may return this book to the Publisher for a complete refund of the price of the book.

Contents

Part One

CHAPTER	TITLE	PAGE
1	The Question I Asked	1
2	The Most Important Thing	5
3	The "Right" Answers	9
4	The Aspects of Self	11
5	The Statement You Make	13
6	Magicians	15
7	The Good News	21
8	Turning Points	29
9	Gift or Curse	31
10	Constructive or Destructive	33
11	This Thing Called Love	35
12	Your Highest Value	37
13	So-called Codependency	41
14	Controlling with Guilt	43
15	Alternative to Selfishness	49
16	Picking and Choosing	53
17	Boulders, Rocks and Sand	63
18	To Bake a Cake, or Not	65
19	Polishing Your Trophy	67
20	Never Powerless	71
21	Deferral, But Not Forever	75
22	The Most Common Drug of Choice	77
23	The Buried Will Rise Again	79

Contents

24	Your Priority Relationship	87
25	Explaining The Attraction	91
26	Onward to the Flame	93
27	Your First Survival Tool	97
28	Why We Need Anger	99
29	The Safe Haven	101
30	Saying Good Bye	105
31	Celebration	109
32	Fear	111
33	Your Second Survival Tool	113
34	Alternatives Only In Theory	117
35	Free Will	119
36	Summary	121

Part Two

37	Beliefs Reflect Our Truth	123
38	Opinions, Beliefs and Convictions	127
39	Core Belief Number One	129
40	Our Earliest Programming	133
41	Unpredictable Outcomes	137
42	Evaluation Defined	139
43	Pre-language	143
44	Leveling the Field	149
45	Emotions, First or Second	151
46	Stress Sources	157
47	Percentages of Reality	161
48	Consciousness, Above and Below	167

An Ultimate Truth

49	Beliefs, Above and Below	171
50	Hidden Drivers	173
51	Action Beliefs	175
52	Core Beliefs	181
53	Common Dysfunctional Beliefs	187
54	The Killer Belief	191
55	Origins of Your Love	197
56	Times to Question	205
57	How to Change Your Beliefs	211

Part Three

58	Dangerous Thinking	217
59	Delivering Information	221
60	Bursting The Bubble	225
61	Too Much Empathy	227
62	Differences of Opinion	229
63	The Risks of Forgiveness	233
64	Letting It Out	241
65	Perchance to Dream	247
66	Change or Cope	249
67	Ten/eighty/ten	251
68	Unearned Guilt	255
69	Say It, Don't Ask	259
70	Six Seconds of Rolling Reality	263
71	Vigilance	267
	Epilogue	273
	Index	277

Introduction — Preview

"Every morning, for more than two years, I woke up with no certainty that I would live to see the following morning. My only absolute certainty came from the knowledge that I could get out of the pain if it got too bad. I always knew the exact location of my loaded handgun. I had fantastic support and the best help imaginable. I deeply appreciated every bit of it. But I appreciated the certainty of a way out even more. If I really had to, if I couldn't handle the agony any more, I knew that I could stop the hurting by tugging on a little metal trigger. Knowing that I had an alternative to the screaming in my head made it possible to think about trying for another day. I spent every day this way for about 750 days straight."

I started my therapeutic mental health practice in 1960 with just one, totally screwed up client. With one like him, I could never have handled more. The experience I just described to you about needing an absolute way out for such a long time occurred many years after I started working with him. In those early years I had a lot to learn. My client helped me in many ways. He forced me to learn things at a great rate because I had to somehow keep ahead of him.

We worked very, very hard together for decades. He drove me to soak up information and experience like the desert under a rain shower. I eventually shared what I had learned with other people. I discovered that they benefited from it. My first client started to improve as well.

He and I went through a lot together, much of it unspeakably painful. Today, my first client and I can look directly into each other's eyes and smile warmly but sadly at each other. Mirrors make things like that possible.

Most intellectual and emotional dysfunction doesn't kill us off immediately. It usually keeps us on the edge of the abyss for a while: sometimes for years, often for a lifetime. Some of us

An Ultimate Truth

terminate our dysfunction in institutions, jails or graves. But, the vast majority of us hang in there and suffer.

Mental retardation and developmental disability affect a small *minority* of the world's population. I do not address, nor have I ever addressed, these afflictions in my practice. They require their own, unique, methods of treatment. However, **some** degree of dysfunction affects the great *majority* of us. A *lesser* degree of dysfunction always reduces the quality of our life. A *greater* degree of dysfunction, in addition to reducing the quality and/or the length of our life, often accompanies mental illness. Those suffering primarily from a diagnosable mental illness, as defined in the American Psychiatric Association's D.S.M.-IV, also require their own, unique, methods of treatment, which lie outside the scope of this book. For the vast majority of us whose dysfunction has **not** yet become incidental to a primary, diagnosed, debilitating, mental illness, I offer a treatment plan that works. We also require our own, unique, therapeutic process.

I had desperately wanted help for my own dysfunction. More than anything, I wanted information and guidance that I could count on and trust. I never found it. So I had to study, research, experience and, in many cases, create sources of insight and information for my own survival. Ultimately, like so many others, I chose to devote myself to providing what I never had to other people. If I had uncovered the information in this book when I first needed it, I could have avoided years of skull-crushing emotional pain.

I had to formulate and create many of the therapeutic models you will come across in the text because they didn't exist anywhere else. I needed them to help my Self first. They have also helped my clients for quite a few years and now I can offer them to you. On the day I learned that my younger brother had killed himself, I vowed that I would publish what I had learned and developed. I never got to share with him what I will share with you in the pages ahead. I want to prevent you from having to experience the same kind of lonely, desperate search that I went through

Introduction — Preview

in my time of greatest need. I want to give you something you can count on and trust.

I have boiled down my years of lectures, courses and training sessions into the chapters which follow. Each chapter could easily expand into a book of its own and that may happen in the future. In every paragraph, I have aimed at brevity, accuracy, passion and precision.

In my opinion, getting **in** to recovery all too often takes on all the characteristics of an unhealthy status symbol. It now has all the appeal, at least in this country, that getting 'in' to psychoanalysis or 'in' to therapy had during years long past.

The philosophies of some recovery programs, particularly those built around twelve levels of progress, have helped perpetuate the myth that an individual's recovery process, once initiated, can never end.

Once we build, or more appropriately **re**build, a house, we have completed the construction process. After the work ends, we certainly can't ignore its upkeep or its maintenance. We need to remain vigilant about our property. We need to constantly watch out for vandals, robbers and acts of nature which could undermine our foundation. But, the fact remains that we have finished the work. The construction crews have gone home for good. **The house stands completed.**

We **can** complete our recovery. Of course we must remain vigilant if we want to maintain what we have built. That applies to everything a human creates. However, after we have gotten **in** to recovery and have done the hard work, we can get **out** of our dysfunction. We can then legitimately refer to our Selves as 'recover**ed**.'

I find the notion of having to exist in a perpetual state of recovery repugnant, unrealistic, fantasy-based, destructive and unnecessary. I have recover**ed**. My wife has recover**ed**. More of my clients than I can keep track of have recover**ed**. Not surprisingly, every one of us chooses to maintain our vigilance in order

An Ultimate Truth

to continuously protect what we have fought so hard to achieve. You can join the ranks of the recovered. You do not have to remain trapped in the recovery process for the rest of your life. You **can** look back from some point in your future and say that you have definitely recovered from your dysfunction. You will then have the ability to honestly and proudly say that you no longer need to hide in the jungle of destructive fantasies.

Speaking of fantasies, in our quest to end the suffering of our dysfunction, and frequently out of desperation, we often turn to sources rooted in warm, fuzzy fantasies. Why not? If nothing else works, of course we will try anything. I have seen so many people extend the sorrow of their dysfunction for years and years by trying to escape into a mystical fantasy world that offered a quick fix. The idea of a short cut has a lot of appeal, especially when nothing else has worked.

We can all escape our dysfunction by diving into the deep waters of magic, mysticism and destructive fantasies. You could. I could. We can always take a short hit of the supernatural and mood alter for a while, at least until the novelty wears off. What then? Either we have to find some new grails to pursue or stop and face the pain within us. We can spend an entire lifetime hopping from one fantasy-distraction to another in order to avoid confronting our pain. If we do that, and so many of us do, we will take the one and only life we have and bury it alive in our own grave. It never had a chance. It never sang the song that only it could have sung if it had grown and developed. No other song will ever duplicate the one that **you** could have sung. You had a once-in-eternity opportunity to fully reveal the unique person buried under your dysfunction. And, you may have chosen to keep it buried under the fluff, smoke and mirrors of mysticism, magic, fantasy and denial. Thus, you could have murdered the most valuable life you have ever known with the weapon of neglect.

We don't need magic, mysticism or destructive fantasies in order to experience recovery. We don't need gurus selling secrets to the chosen few. We do need clear, simple truth and we need

Introduction — Preview

instructions on how to apply it rationally, realistically and constructively to our Selves.

Every bit of information and every experience of your life has trained and educated you for this moment. If "this moment" contains the emotional pain, misery and suffering of dysfunction; if it contains stress or so-called codependency, bouts of depression or anxiety, self destructive or addictive/compulsive behavior, then one of your options involves getting new training to empower you to overcome the old training. That simple, but difficult process takes a lot of work. It requires instruction, guidance and direction from someone who has experienced what you have experienced, felt what you have felt and learned, from what they went through, how to survive and permanently recover.

One of the most destructive consequences of our past training, from birth till now, manifests in our programming to accept the unacceptable, the intolerable, the uncomfortable and the Self destructive as defensible and somehow appropriate. To overcome a lifetime of past training requires present retraining, different training, healthier training, better training than we ever had before. We need new information, new instructions and new guidance. *We need to learn what we couldn't possibly have known before. If we had gotten the information when we needed it, our dysfunction would **not** have afflicted us in the first place.*

If you've had enough; if you want to take full responsibility for the quality of your own life; if independence has more importance to you than dependence; if you can visualize your real identity, but can't quite get there; if you have the courage to work hard because the person buried inside you, under the dysfunction, really does matter; if you have an intense determination to celebrate your one and only reality rather than to suffer from it and if you want to take charge of an unmanageable life, then I wrote this book for you. No one should have to suffer from lack of information the way so many of us did.

PART ONE

1
The Question I Asked

I asked a terrible question.

Does a simple statement of truth exist with which every human who has ever lived, past or present, could voluntarily agree?

Of course I would have to assume that whoever heard the statement could hear it in their own language and that they would have enough intellectual capacity to understand it.

The statement would have to deliver a clear, acceptable message to any person, anywhere, anytime in history.

Every member of every religion; the non-religious; the atheists; the agnostics; every culture and every ethnic group that exists, or ever existed, would have to feel comfortable voluntarily embracing the statement without reservation.

What possible reason could I have had, other than a complete loss of sanity, for asking such a crazy question in the first place?

I had a very strong personal reason to attempt to find a common ground. My clients, my students and my audiences all came from diverse philosophical backgrounds. Where could we begin the process of negotiating knowledge? Where could we stand, together, to begin our journey? On what could we willingly and voluntarily agree every time we talked with each other?

I began a search for a rational starting point that would feel comfortable for all of us. I wanted something that we could agree upon completely. I needed a solid foundation for us to build upon.

I accepted the challenge, from myself, to create something with which **every** person on the face of the earth could voluntarily agree.

An Ultimate Truth

Could such a thing even exist? I very quickly began to think that I had bitten off a bit more than anyone in their right mind could chew.

The concept of an "Ultimate Truth" has historically generated endless controversy. Every apparently universal truth always seems to give birth to a whole new family of contradictory assertions. To most people truth, like ethics, appears dependent upon the expediency of the moment. One person's truth seems to inevitably wind up defining another person's untruth.

I thought I had an answer by the tail with the "Golden Rule." It even looked like a universal truth. It kept showing up during most periods of world history. I started keeping track of what I found. You might find these paraphrases interesting. *Confucianism, in the sixth century BCE gave us, "What you don't want done to yourself, don't do to others." From Buddhism in the fifth century BCE we got, "Hurt not others with what pains yourself." Also in the fifth century BCE, Jainism gave us the longest version, "In happiness and in suffering, in joy and in grief, we should regard all creatures as we regard our selves. We should therefore refrain from inflicting upon others such injury as would appear undesirable to us if inflicted upon ourselves." Again, in the fifth century BCE, we got, "Do not do unto others that which bodes not well for oneself," from Zoroastrianism. Plato gave us, "May I do unto others what I would wish them to do unto me," in the fourth century BCE. In the third century BCE, the Hindu Mahabharata provided us with, "Do nothing to others which, if done to you, would cause you pain." In the first century BCE, Rabbi Hillel purportedly said, "Don't do to your fellow man what would seem hateful for you to receive." In the first century AD, Christianity gave us, "Whatsoever you would that men should do unto you, do you also unto them." In the nineteenth century AD, Chief Joseph of the Nez Perce said, "Our fathers gave us many laws which they learned from their fathers. They told us to treat all men as they treated us."*

The Question I Asked

All these statements still failed to solve my problem. Too many people could rationally disagree with even these benign and benevolent utterances. For example, **you** could rationally disagree because your own experience has taught you that treating other people the way you want them to treat you doesn't always work. It may work **sometimes**, but it doesn't work **all** the time. I guarantee that you have treated at least one person in your life with kindness only to have that person respond to you with **un**kindness.

It appeared that I had assigned myself an impossible task by taking on this search for common ground. Almost impossible; I preoccupied myself with the problem for more than two years.

Nowadays, when speaking with groups or individuals, I often ask them to try to come up with a statement of their own that they believe would answer the question. I regularly give my clients the challenge as an assignment.

And I will *not* share the result of my quest with you just yet. I would like to suggest that you take on the assignment yourself. It took me two years. I would like to ask you to consider investing a few minutes. Remember, if one person can rationally disagree with the statement you come up with, you have to start over again.

An Ultimate Truth

2
The Most Important Thing

Please hold on to whatever you came up with and walk with me for a while.

I have trained and counseled people for over thirty five years in the mental health field. I have specialized in teaching people how to survive dysfunction and prevent it from killing them. I earned the title of "my first client." I had to learn how to save my own life and sanity first. What I learned, I shared. What I continue to learn, I will continue to share.

One fact has beaten me over the head with its certainty, year after year, with client after client. Every breathing human walking around has a list in their heads that calls all the shots. That list represents and comprises a belief system.

A few "core" beliefs in this system control thousands of "action beliefs." Action beliefs generate 100% of our choices. Our choices generate 100% of our voluntary actions. Our beliefs also give rise to virtually all of our emotions. Our beliefs will determine whether we will perceive stress as a positive or a negative experience. I will share a lot more about this with you later on.

Your list, and the beliefs engraved upon it, directs all your actions, activates almost all of your emotions and determines the type of stress you will experience. I think that makes those beliefs vitally important and yet most people have no idea what their own list, their own belief system, looks like.

I would like to ask you to identify just one core belief from your own list. I'll make it easy for you. I will ask you a specific question in order to lead you towards that particular belief on your own, unique list.

Question: of all the realities that you could imagine or experience, which one, above all the others, seems the most impor-

An Ultimate Truth

tant to you? Which one would you fight to retain? Which one would you refuse to relinquish?

Please consider your response carefully. I recognize that many important things exist in your world. I challenge you to come up with **your** number one, not anyone else's. Let other people provide their own answer to the question. As it happens, that will occur automatically anyway. Everyone does, in fact, come up with their own answer, either purposefully or accidentally; with or without awareness.

In other words, what exists for you as the most important thing your senses can perceive?

As you can imagine, over the years people have come up with quite a variety of answers. They tend to range from spouse, family or happiness to their work or their gods. Probably the most frequent reply refers to children or grandchildren as number one.

At this point, I usually reformat the question as a statement. Name the one thing without which all the other important things would seem meaningless to you. If you don't have **it**, you couldn't have any of the other things of relatively lesser importance.

One word of advice: think simply. Try not to think in terms of something complicated.

What ever you have chosen for your answer identifies your most significant core belief, affecting more of your choices, emotions and actions than any other belief on your list.

If what I will respectfully offer you differs from what you came up with on your own, please seriously reconsider your answer and reevaluate the thought process that led up to your conclusion.

YOU, YOUR LIFE, YOUR EXISTENCE identifies the most important thing you know. Without your life, within which you perceive all the other important things, you would have no ability whatsoever to appreciate and prioritize anything else that you see as valuable, worthwhile or significant. You have **got** to have **it** first.

The Most Important Thing

If your answer named your partner, how could you express your high regard, love and value for him/her if you did not first exist? The same applies to your children or your grandchildren. If you value and love them, you can't show that love to them if you do not exist. You can't protect that which you value without first manifesting your own presence.

You've got to have your own life first. All the rest comes second in priority. Even if you want to sacrifice your life for somebody else, you have to possess that life in the first place before you can give it away. Sacrifice requires you to exchange a higher value (you) for another, relatively lesser value (the other). Exchanging a lower value for a higher value doesn't fit the proper definition of sacrifice. It fits the definition of a good deal and a bargain. That which you perceive as worthy of the highest value you can assign to anything defines **you**.

Spirituality, a sense of connectedness to something greater than ourselves, becomes meaningless and impossible without the existence of your life necessarily preceding an awareness of that connection.

You, the most important, valuable entity within your awareness! Your life, the most valuable thing you know!

If you can comfortably accept this premise, then the next question will sound like this. How do you treat that which you consider valuable? In other words, when someone gives you a gift that you value, how do you handle it? What do you do with it?

If you received the most valuable gem in the world as a gift, you would probably insure it and place it in a vault, fast!

When you buy a new car or a house, you immediately protect your investment with insurance. You insure your life in order to protect others from the economic losses they would suffer due to your death. Everyone has a special possession that has no monetary value whatsoever: perhaps a gift from a special person or a reminder of a treasured occasion. These items rest in safe

An Ultimate Truth

keeping, sometimes for many years. They have value in the eyes of the holder. Because they have value, they receive protection.

Important things have great value **for** us. We value most highly those things that we perceive as the most important. We will always act to protect that which we value. If we don't value something, we won't protect it. Value-less equals protection-less.

Your life, the most valuable thing you know. Maybe, maybe not. In what ways do you protect your most valuable asset? In what ways do you protect the most valuable thing you know? A created human entity has to protect, develop and celebrate its one and only life. A created human entity: that means us, you and me.

3
The "Right" Answers

Identifying whatever created you falls into the lap of theology and religion. Theology sets up the big picture while religion applies the philosophy of a particular theology to the daily life of its followers. Each of us chooses the name(s) and the nature(s) of that which appears greater than ourselves. You choose your theology and your religion as a result of a very private process. No one else's nose belongs in your business when you make your choice. In my practice I concern myself very deeply with spirituality, defined as a sense of connectedness with something greater than ourselves. I do not concern myself with other people's theology or religion. Religion concerns itself with labels, procedures and interpretations. The mission of any religion consists of creating rituals; putting faces, names and labels on its gods and attempting to explain the unexplainable. Hundreds of different theological systems exist today. Thousands of them have existed, and disappeared, in the past. Every one of them, past or present, claimed or claims to have the only "right" answers. Most of them label those who adhere to other theologies as heretics. The overwhelming contradictions inherent among conflicting theologies often destroys spirituality. It becomes impossible to feel any sense of connectedness to something greater when **my** something greater has to represent a choice among so many sincere, but different, representations of something greater.

This theological jungle of confusion and contradiction contributes to dysfunction. The truth of this manifests in the reasonable statement, "They can't **all** have the 'right' answer!" If we choose one religion to follow from amongst the many, members of the ones we didn't pick will pity us for our stupidity or condemn us for our heresy. If we choose none, we lose access to our spirituality. If we choose them all, we lose our connection with reality.

An Ultimate Truth

An interesting footnote: what does the opposite of believing in **something** look like?

Most people would answer, "Believing in **nothing**."

In the world of religion and theology, the opposite of believing in something often takes the form of believing in **everything**.

If we choose one particular religion as the source of our spirituality, we will have to dig ourselves into it deeply, profoundly and zealously. We will have to aggressively observe its rituals and sacraments. We will have to proclaim its dogma and its doctrine loudly and passionately. Our cosmology will have to represent the **only** cosmology. Our deity, or deities, will have to stand alone. Our sacred writings will have to represent the **only** authority on the subject. Our doctrine, our rites and customs, our explanations of the unknown, our rituals and our ceremonies will all have to define the **only** pathway to peace of mind and happiness. We will have to dismiss any other point of view as erroneous and misguided.

If we don't vigorously throw ourselves into the religion of our choice, we might have troubling doubts and nightmarish fears. Questioning the particular theological system we have chosen could lead to the loss of our peace of mind. We could lose our ready answers to all the mysteries of existence. The known could revert to the unknown. We could feel ignorant, frightened, vulnerable and isolated. We could find our Selves surrounded by unanswered mysteries.

The situation could turn into a classic can't / must conflict. I **must** have a religion in order to know how to experience my sense of connectedness to something greater than myself but I **can't** resolve the fact that decent, caring people from the religions I *didn't* pick will tell me I made the wrong choice.

And, to make matters worse, they will tell me I made the wrong choice with furrowed brows, troubled hearts, honest conviction and deep sincerity. Once again, we can't **all** have the 'right' answers, can we?

4

The Aspects of Self

This seemingly unresolvable dilemma doesn't help my dysfunctional clients, it only adds to their pain and their confusion.

Dysfunction of the person, of the Self, does not mean **non**-function because we can still operate at some level, no matter how minimal. The Greek prefix "dys" means "abnormal" or "defective." We just can't operate as well as we used to. I often ask clients to point to a time in their life when they believe they truly experienced full functionality. I get many different answers. The most appropriate ones refer to the time shortly after we first came into the world. The one and only time we experienced **all** the characteristics of a fully functional human organism occurred at the moment of and shortly after our birth, before outside factors could begin to influence us. Emotional dysfunction in a parent, or parents, can afflict a developing fetus long before the moment of birth. For most of us however, the downhill slide began as we emerged into our brand new, but dysfunctional, environment.

When we refer to the Self, exactly what do we describe? When we refer to a person or to a human, to what exactly do we refer? I suggest that at least four aspects, or facets, of the Self exist. I suggest that first, we have a physical reality. We can easily touch and feel our own bodies. Second, we have our intellect: our ability to think, our intelligence, our ability to perceive. Third, we have our ability to experience our emotions. Fourth, we have our spirituality, our sense of connectedness to something greater than our Selves.

Obviously, when the term dysfunction applies to the body it means that something physical does not work as originally intended. Any examples I offer you will necessarily assume that the body operates functionally; that physically everything works. Clearly, a dysfunctioning body will impact the other three aspects.

An Ultimate Truth

Conversely, dysfunction in any of the other three parts will certainly effect the body, eventually if not immediately.

To summarize, your Self and my Self consist of four primary aspects: physical, intellectual, emotional and spiritual. Our responsibility as created beings requires us to protect, develop and celebrate this Self. Dysfunction means operating at anything less than full capacity in any of the four aspects of the Self. The effect of dysfunction shows up in our inability to carry out our responsibility as caretaker, protector, developer, defender and celebrant of the one and only life that rests completely in our own hands.

5

The Statement You Make

Let's return to the question I asked you earlier. Hopefully you came up with a statement, or statements, that you felt could receive universal acceptance.

How did you do? How did it go? Did it seem easy or hard? Did you, in fact, come up with anything at all?

Did you think that you had "it" and then experience deep disappointment because just one person could rationally disagree?

I hope so. I hope you got a small taste of the frustration involved in such an assignment.

Please keep any notes you may have made. I predict that you may want to share them with someone you love, value and care for at some time in your future.

You'll probably want to make them sweat a little, just like you did.

A clue: the statement that I came up with has six words, begins with "I," ends with "myself" and has "not" as the third word.

With that information, would you please take some more time to try to come up with something on your own? I promise I won't leave you hanging much longer.

Actually, the first time I really thought I had "it" occurred when I devised a statement that contained only five words.

It stood, unchallenged, for quite a while, until a member of a lecture audience rationally disagreed with it. I dragged my bruised ego back to the drawing board and eventually came up with the six word statement I referred to that, incidentally, has stood successfully against all subsequent challenges.

An Ultimate Truth

6

Magicians

Earlier, I referred to the term "existence." Vague and vaporous images automatically swirl around that word. We have two opposing definitions of existence to deal with, one rational and one mystical. The rational definition of "existence" wraps around the six word statement I keep dangling in front of you. The mystical approach to existence, which you won't find in anything I share with you, requires some commentary nonetheless.

Mysticism comprises fantasy, magic and the chosen few; those who know versus those who don't; us versus them; obscurity and uncertainty; lack of definition and clarity. Magicians of the mind use all these tools and more. They rely on the idea that something spiritual **must** require interpretation. They promote the magician-interpreter as the only person capable of unraveling the threads of the thing that needs the interpretation. They have to make sure that we see them as the only mediator between us and the unknown.

Two of the most significant systems in our lives, the family system and the religious system, have great appeal to the magician mentality. Many things in both systems lack clear definitions. Lots of questions float around without answers. Answers don't reveal themselves easily or at all. An interpreter will gladly help the poor, confused members of either system achieve some degree of understanding and some level of comfort with the unknown.

Parents become the interpreters of the secrets within the family system, of course; the very same parents who, in many cases, have created, or at the very least perpetuated, most of the family's secrets in the first place.

The interpreters of religions also tend to create the very secrets they purport to explain. That seems reasonable, since their power derives from interpreting mysteries.

An Ultimate Truth

A vast difference separates a legitimate mystery from mysticism.

A genuine mystery generates legitimate questions. And, horror of horrors, some of those legitimate questions simply don't have any answers.

Mysticism must generate questions that have as many different answers as possible. Every question has to have some kind of answer, no matter how obscure. Genuine mysteries make magician-interpreters nervous. Interpreters with unexplained mysteries on their hands lose their influence over people, so they perpetuate as many mysteries as they can.

Mysticism can manifest itself within any group of people. Create an appealing mystical system and you can gain power and control over the group. It has always worked this way.

Incidentally, you can create a successful mystical, religious, philosophical, economic or judicial system if you just follow certain steps. I look forward to having you appreciate the irony.

First, make sure that obscurity and lack of clarity characterize your policies, procedures, rituals, ceremonies, rites, customs, rules, laws, practices, dogma, liturgy, creed and central beliefs.

Second, guarantee that none of the above makes any sense without interpretation. Make sure that only you, or your collaborators, have the keys necessary to decipher the codes you have created. Ideally, you will appoint yourself the Messenger or the Prophet of the Deity or Deities you create. You should make certain that you appear as merely a 'humble' servant of the Great and Mystical.

Third, make certain that the other people you engage as interpreters appear hard to find. Create a mystique around their special attributes and qualities. Emphasize how hard you have to search to locate them. Foster the impression that such people only come forward in response to a deep, inner calling. Cultivate their image as truly unique individuals.

Magicians

Fourth, see to it that only a small group of very special people; the select few; the chosen; the initiates; the inner circle; can even partly understand the words of the interpreters. Say that those who already understand require no explanations and that those who don't understand could not possibly comprehend the explanations. Make sure that outsiders perceive membership in your group as an extraordinary personal achievement.

Fifth, demand complete, blind acceptance of every aspect of your mystical system from your membership. Give such an unquestioning, undoubting and unchallenging attitude the label of "faith." Ostracize those who do not accept your system on faith.

Sixth, devote most of your personal energies to your elite minority rather than to the majority who have yet to see the greatness of your system. The enthusiastic, convicted, chosen few will effectively draw the uncertain, prospective converts into your cause.

Seventh, make sure that you present the philosophy of your mystical creation as the one and only truth. Consistently and aggressively characterize all other systems as false.

Eighth, always see to it that your believers perceive the group's experience as infinitely superior to the personal experience of any one individual.

Ninth, present, as an absolute certainty, the notion that every human breathing has the latent potential to elevate themselves to a level worthy of consideration for membership in your organization but that only a very special few will have the insight and the ability to really understand, fully appreciate and ultimately join your exclusive group.

Tenth, above all, create a new language! Make sure that you concoct words that have never existed before or give new interpretations to old words. Make certain that only those of your inner circle know the new, esoteric meanings. Make it difficult for outsiders to obtain translations of your new lingo. Make your initiates endlessly commit new words and phrases to memory without understanding them. Later, you can occasionally reward them with a definition, thereby raising them, in their own minds, one rung further up the ladder which leads to the inner circle. If you can control the language of your mystical undertaking you can easily control your victims.

Once your mystical entity begins to function, you will have all kinds of opportunities to proclaim to one and all the "spiritual" nature of your enterprise. Make sure that you proclaim it loudly and often. Spirituality can appear to have supplanted mysticism if you have done your work adroitly. You can cloak the obfuscations of your mystical creation with warm, fuzzy references to "Higher planes of Spiritual experience." You can hide your desire for power and control over people under the facade of leading them to a place of greater spiritual insight and fulfillment.

I once heard some people interviewed about something unusual and mysterious they thought they had seen. They all had strong feelings about what they believed they had just viewed. They each expressed awe as they described their experience. One person said that, **"I felt chosen!** No one else could possibly have had my experience. **What I saw made me feel so special: sort of singled out from other people.** I know that my life has moved into a new dimension. I no longer feel like the same person." If you play your cards right and follow the list I just gave you, you will develop the ability to elicit the same kind of heartfelt, fantasy fulfilling response to *your* mystical endeavor.

I often get phone calls from people inquiring about my practice. Occasionally, the caller will ask a question that sounds something like this: "Do you use a spiritual approach to help people through their recovery?"

On the surface, the question sounds sincere. However, experience has provided insight as to the caller's true intent. The real message sounds like this:

Magicians

I do not want to accept responsibility for my Self.

I do not want to accept responsibility for my actions or my choices.

I want a magical short cut that will enable me to remain irresponsible and unaccountable.

I want a short cut that involves little or no work on my part.

I want a god or gods to do my work for me.

I want he, she, it or them to do a miracle for me.

If it doesn't work, I want something other than myself to blame it on.

An Ultimate Truth

7

The Good News

A very fine line separates profound agreement from profound disagreement. Below that line, everybody agrees with each other. Above the line, nobody can agree with anybody.

The statement that I searched for and wanted everyone to agree with lies below the line.

I hope you have invested some real effort in coming up with a statement of your own. I'll assume that you have and share my six word answer to the question with you now. Here it comes.

I did not completely create myself.

My first solution omitted the word 'completely.' A student in the audience rightly pointed out how some religions maintain that, in between lives, believers spend their time evaluating and ultimately choosing their next parents. In my defense, I really had known that, but it slipped through the cracks. These individuals feel, to some degree, responsible for their own creation and therefore could not voluntarily agree with my original statement. Changing the statement by adding the word 'completely' resolved the conflict. A person could feel 99.9% responsible for their own creation if they wished, but the remaining percentage **had** to originate externally. No one woke up one morning and said "I think that I'll create myself today." So far, no one has come forward willing to claim that they have **totally** self-created. Even those waiting for rebirth would eventually require the miracle of a biological birth to complete their next incarnation. No one has, as yet, claimed to have self-birthed.

An Ultimate Truth

I did not completely create myself. **Something** else had to exist in order to complete my creation, regardless of the part, large or small, I may believe it played in the process.

I did not create me: bad language but an inescapable conclusion.

I did not completely create myself, the statement below the line, the one that everyone can rationally agree with.

Above the line however, we have another story altogether. Above the line nobody can agree with anybody. Total conflict and disagreement prevails.

Question: what changed as we crossed the line? Below the line we have the potential for complete, universal agreement with no conflicts. Above the line we have *nothing but* conflict, disagreement and chaos.

Answer: labels. Below the line, everyone conceded that **something** other than ourselves ran loose in the universe. They also allowed that without that something, we couldn't exist; that something had to either initiate or complete the act of creation, we couldn't do the job alone. We needed *it*.

Everyone seemed content with terms such as 'it' and 'something.' Such neutral words make no demands upon the imagination. They represent a true mystery: something that comfortably precludes further definition.

Unless, of course, we do not remain content with the mystery. Then we **really** get into trouble and start to feel uncomfortable.

If we feel compelled to go further and cross the line into the world of labels, what consequences occur? What discomforts, conflicts and chaos do we experience?

Suddenly, peace disappears. A Satisfying contentment with a mystery no longer exists. We need answers! We need labels! We must have a face to put upon the unknown. Leaving the mystery alone only generates a deep discontentment.

The Good News

Once we have crossed the line, searching everywhere and anywhere for answers to the mystery, turmoil, confusion and disorder prevail. **Now, everybody disagrees, about everything!**

Consider the amount of life energy wasted, throughout human history, as a result of the conflict between those who disagree. Consider the unspeakable tragedy represented by the uncountable and irreplaceable lives consumed by violent disagreements over theological concepts. Consider the deaths beyond measure attributable to so called 'Holy' wars and inquisitions, in virtually every period of history and in every culture on the face of the earth. Genocide ultimately determines the dominance of one system's set of labels over another. The reasonable statement, "They can't all have the 'right' answer," translates into the madness of, "My way or no way!" The latter statement usually delivers its final punctuation mark by putting holes into the people who disagree, with spears, rocks, arrows, knives, bullets or bombs.

How comfortable can **you** feel with a genuine, insolvable mystery on your hands? Most people seem very **un**comfortable. They demand answers, regardless of the absurdity of those answers. They must have answers at any cost. A horror of the unknown, any unknown, seems to overwhelm them.

What colossal arrogance to presume the ability to know every answer to every question. Normally, only deities suffer the attribution of omniscience and, of course, they disagree among themselves.

Consider an expert in any field. Visualize anyone you wish, past or present. Make certain that, in your mind, they stand at the absolute pinnacle of their specialty. Interestingly, what they **don't** know, about everything, will add up to infinitely more than what they **do** know, about anything. What you or I know, what we really, actually factually know about anything falls like a drop of water into an ocean of that which we do not know.

We can and do hold opinions of course, on everything. However, opinions do not define reality. Reality defines itself,

An Ultimate Truth

without our help or permission. What exists, exists, whether I like it or not and whether I know it or not.

One's opinions and fantasies do not automatically translate into facts. Opinions have no basis in certainty. Opinions well researched may evolve into new, factual discoveries, but only after surviving the purifying process of a deep and penetrating series of challenges.

The original question again: how comfortable can you feel with a genuine mystery?

What alternatives do you have? You can have a narrow, fanatical zeal with blinders or a belief in everything or a belief in nothing. You pick it.

Or, you can have a belief in the truth and the wonder of an incredible mystery **as a mystery**, which no one can satisfactorily explain.

Must I have every answer and every label from one, or every, theological system in the universe before I can allow my Self to appreciate that which I can directly understand and personally experience? Must I perpetually chase what does *not* exist instead of reveling in the glory of that which *does* exist?

The beauty of a sunset fades by comparison with the magnificence of the fact that we have the capacity to appreciate it in the first place. The sublime sunset would still illuminate the earth even if we did not exist. Our ability to appreciate supersedes the beauty of that which we have the capacity to perceive.

Birth, life, death; no one belief system has a monopoly on the definitions of these absolutely universal experiences. 100% of humans experience these three phenomena, and virtually 100% of them disagree as to how and why they occur.

In similar fashion, people use the equipment of technology every day without, for the most part, understanding exactly how or why it works, unless they happen to have designed the apparatus in the first place.

The Good News

Most people appreciate the value of the equipment they use and they don't have arguments with each other about the mysteries of the mechanisms. In short, they accept the mystery and appreciate the value of it in their experience.

You have never heard someone refuse to benefit from technology solely because they did not fully understand how the thing works.

Would you refuse to use a simple piece of equipment, like a telephone, just because you didn't know exactly how and why it works, in complete technical detail? Of course not. You just go ahead and use it.

Most machinery looks mysterious to most people. Fortunately, a lack of understanding on our part doesn't preclude utilization. If it did, we would never have evolved past the stone age.

The ability to accept and appreciate a mystery, what an extraordinary basis for a theological system. Such a system would not need any interpreters. Nothing would require interpretation. Its members would all voluntarily agree that, past a certain point, they just don't have any answers, and neither does anyone else. They could easily agree that lacking all the answers does not make them uncomfortable.

Members of this theological system would have the freedom, the ability, and the power, to worship, proclaim, praise, revere, venerate and thank a wonderful, nameless, faceless Power, that exists beyond anyone's understanding, for all that they **can** experience and appreciate.

No personification of the unknown Power would occur. No assignment of gender, such as labels of him or her, would have any reason to show up either.

Any member of this system could easily, happily and reasonably spend their entire life expressing profound gratitude for their consciousness and their existence.

We may not know the exact, universally acceptable form of the crea**tor** but we definitely know the form of the crea**ted**. Just

An Ultimate Truth

look in a mirror. We appear as the marvelous and incredible handiwork of something unknown to any of us creations. I strongly suggest that we accept the mystery **as a mystery**. No requirement exists anywhere in reality for us to cross the line into the world of labels in order to feel the joy of celebration and worship.

Observe your complete Self, your physical, intellectual, emotional and spiritual Self. The act of looking requires the engagement of your internal and external senses, and your consciousness. The Self requires an existence to recognize in the first place and a consciousness to recognize it in the second place. You have awareness of your Self. You experience Self-awareness. Your Self exists. Your awareness exists. You possess the two, absolutely essential, attributes of human reality: consciousness and existence.

This last statement does **not** express a postulate that rests upon unproven assumptions or that relies upon faith for its support. Quite the contrary, it rests upon the unshakable foundation of reason and experience. No faith required. You exist! You have consciousness of your existence!

On these two pillars, a true philosophy of recovery and celebration can rise to exalt the human spirit **and** the nameless, faceless Power as well, with no interpretation required from the magicians.

A wonderful mystery exists, and your Self can become a part of it. Your unique, human component can merge with a great, mysterious ocean of reality and, rather than experience diminishment or any loss of Self, your identity can **gain** the depth of the sea as well as its mystery.

The mystery of the creation of life; the mystery of life itself; the mystery of death, all of these great unknowns and more make up the nature of the reality we can join.

Death, for example. As far as we know, the human species has an awareness of its own mortality that no other living creature possesses. We alone know that death awaits us. Apparently no other living entity has this forewarning.

The Good News

Knowledge of our eventual termination results in a lifetime of coping, in many different ways. Some deny it any room in their thoughts. Others leap to embrace an afterlife, with or without the help of a religion. Some die a thousand deaths while living, due to fear and terror of the possibility of extinction. A few view death as a natural transition and come comfortably to terms with it. Every individual develops their own coping technique. Like religions, most of these techniques conflict with one another. Once again, "They can't all have the 'right' answer." Another of reality's great mysteries, and yet one for which everyone will acquire an answer, eventually.

The energies that became 'us' apparently existed for an eternity before they formed into you and I. When our form has finished with them, the same energies will surely continue into an infinite future. It would seem that we can never truly 'not exist.'

The mystery and the miracle of the creation of life which no human fully understands; that moment of fertilization before which a life form did not exist and after which it does. What an incredible moment, and it happens countless times a second on our dynamic world, taking into account all forms of plant and animal life.

The mystery of life itself: consciousness and existence, the mystery above all mysteries.

We experience mysteries and non-mysteries. I respectfully suggest that we leave the genuine mysteries alone and attempt to achieve some rational level of comfort with them, **as mysteries**. Everyone with whom I have shared this information has returned to their faith or religion more at ease with it than before. Choosing to voluntarily cross the line into a specific theological system of labels and doctrine can result in feeling some additional comfort with the uncertainties of the mysteries. Also, worshipping by choice rather than by indoctrination uplifts the human Spirit. All too soon, the non-mysteries of life will aggressively engage us from every side.

An Ultimate Truth

8

Turning Points

Dysfunction, for example, inflicts a major non-mystery upon us. It creates the pain, the suffering, the torment and the isolation we feel. We have crystal-clear awareness of our misery.

Remember, any **in**ability to fully utilize any aspect of my physical, intellectual, emotional and spiritual Self amounts to a degree of dysfunction. Degrees of dysfunction appear as shades of gray, not all or nothing, black or white extremes. If my dysfunction only nominally manifests itself, my life will flow along fairly smoothly with very few crises. I will probably never hit a major turning point that would require other people to intervene for my own safety or the safety of others. As my dysfunction increases, the likelihood of my banging into more of the walls of life increases. Lower levels of dysfunction generate mild levels of real life discomfort. Moving to higher levels of dysfunction generates increasingly more intense levels of pain, suffering and unhappiness in all four areas of my existence. My dysfunctional experience depends very much on the degree of my affliction. People with very minor dysfunction usually have little or no awareness of their condition. It generally takes the experience of suffering to get their attention.

Nobody asks for help in recovering from dysfunction unless they have experienced a crisis or a turning point. My own experience, as well as the experience of my clients, leads me to characterize those turning points as many faceted.

Perhaps we could have a subtle and gentle experience such as looking in the mirror one day and quietly realizing that we have no knowledge whatsoever of the identity of that person in the mirror. This often activates an overwhelming sense of panic.

We could experience a cataclysmic and dramatic turning point by waking up in jail or in an institution, wired up to life

An Ultimate Truth

support machines with absolutely no knowledge of how we got there.

We could suddenly realize that our many failed relationships couldn't possibly have originated with all those other people and that the responsibility actually rests upon our own shoulders.

Whatever your turning point becomes, if you have yet to hit it, or whatever you have already experienced, I can guarantee that fear either did or will manifest as the dominant emotional state. Fear, the great motivator. Nothing motivates like fear. The second human motivator, a desire to acquire more than we have, will always take a back seat to fear.

The turning point, however it occurs, represents the first stage of recovery.

Secondly, we have to learn how we got this way to start with; what roots lie beneath our dysfunction.

Thirdly, we need new tools and instructions regarding the use of those tools in order to make genuine changes in our physical, intellectual, emotional and spiritual Self. We have to learn how to protect, develop and celebrate that Self.

The fourth stage I call vigilance, maintenance if you prefer. Nothing we can build will continue to stand without taking care of it. How to do that, for the rest of our life, becomes the final stage of genuine recovery.

9

Gift or Curse

Let's go back to the most important thing you know: your own life, your existence. Add to that the universally acceptable concept of, "I did not completely create myself."

Now, if you did not completely create yourself and the process of creation involved **something** greater than yourself, then the most valuable thing you know, your life, could not have emerged from something *you* came up with. You didn't create you, something else did. Stick a label on that 'something' if you must, but you did **not** bring your own life into existence, something else did. Therefore, your life acquires the characteristics of something you **got**, something you **received**, rather than something you created.

Since you received your life, what opinion do you have about it? To what extent do you value what you've got? Do you see your life as a gift, a curse, or as something in between? Do you see your life, the **fact** of your existence, as the most valuable thing you know or as something you can't wait to see come to an end, or something in between? I challenge you to come up with your own answer. Where does your truth lie?

Gift or curse, all of your choices flow from your perception of the value and the worth of your life. If you see your life as a gift, you will celebrate it. If you see it as a curse, you will try to get out from under it. As regards getting out from under it, you have three options.

Option one: you can get away from the curse of life fast, by pulling the trigger or stepping off the ledge. From my experience with clients, I can tell you that the inability to make this particular choice often heaps a sense of personal failure and cowardice on top of the original pain.

An Ultimate Truth

Option two: you can get away from the curse of living by choosing to kill a piece of your Self, physically, intellectually, emotionally or spiritually, every chance you get, every day, every minute if possible. This process usually takes a lifetime. You can gradually destroy the quality of your life this way and, by doing that, slowly kill the thing that you hate.

The third option requires that you establish relationships with people who will enable your Self-execution by performing either option one or option two upon you. That way, you won't have to do it to yourself. In fact, you can even enjoy the luxury of blaming them for your own misery and eventual destruction, as you kill your curse second hand. Your choice to put the power to destroy yourself into their hands can absolve you of any perceived responsibility.

We have to make a choice, day to day, minute by minute, second by second as to whether we live or die. We, as adult humans, do **not** have an automatic instinct for survival. Animals do, we don't. We have to constantly choose between life or death. We can choose non-life just as well as we can choose life. Every choice we make will either move us towards life or towards non-life; towards constructive or destructive; towards positive or negative.

10

Constructive or Destructive

I always try to get my clients to change that part of their thinking, and speaking, vocabulary which assigns labels of 'good' or 'bad', 'right' or 'wrong' to things. These words carry tremendous intellectual and emotional baggage with them. Every person will have different definitions of right and wrong. Finding common ground gets tougher, not easier.

I suggest to them, and to you, that you replace all those words with either 'constructive' or 'destructive' or, in a pinch, 'plus' or 'minus' or 'positive' and 'negative.'

The terms constructive or destructive apply to your choices.

Constructive describes those choices made in favor of your life, which add value to its quality or its length.

Destructive describes choices which take away value from either the quality or the length of your life.

Using these two terms forces great clarity and honesty upon you and me.

If I say that I think you made a destructive choice, I must further refine my statement by spelling out 'to whom' the choice appears destructive.

If I choose to steal your money; constructive for me, destructive for you. Consistently come to work late; constructive for you, destructive for your employer. Let your child get away with murder; constructive for you now, destructive for the kid, and eventually destructive for you both, years down the road.

Try it. See if you can express yourself exclusively in terms of constructive and destructive choices. Also try to identify the

An Ultimate Truth

other people to whom your choices might appear either positive or negative.

Constructive choices: those adding value to the quality or length of your life. Destructive choices: those subtracting value from the quality or length of your life.

Your 'life' includes those people whom you value. Positive and negative choices apply to you and includes them. That which benefits you also benefits them. That which benefits them also benefits you. You share your existence with them.

11

This Thing Called Love

What benefits you, and those you value, brings me to the concept of "selfishness." Every person I have ever worked with has shown evidence of brainwashing on this topic. I'll bet that includes you. I'll prove it to you. I'll play you a tape from your childhood. Complete this statement. "You never think of other people, you just don't care about anyone else, **how can you act so** _____?" Well, what popped into your mind? Sure, **selfishly**. Welcome to the world of childhood preprogramming, that sets early beliefs in concrete.

Our childhood often set us up to believe that the label of 'selfish' branded us completely unlovable, undesirable and totally unacceptable. Most of our parents used it as a tool of control through guilt. Kids behave better when they carry guilt on their back and in their heart. They will frequently not act out on behalf of themselves if they see that Self as undeserving of love and acceptance from those who have all the power.

So the Self gets a bad reputation. Anything we do that gets labeled as 'selfish' causes us to feel that we have somehow lost, or failed to deserve, our parents' love and acceptance. This applies to any other word-concepts that we combine with the Self. They will also suffer from the same stigma.

For example, Self esteem expresses one of my least favorite word-concepts. What does esteem really mean? If I try to convince another person that I really love them, can I say that, "I really 'esteem' you" and get my message across? I don't think so.

If I raise my head to the heavens, or wherever my deities reside, and try to express my praise and worship, and I say, "My god, I 'esteem' you," somehow it doesn't get the message across either.

An Ultimate Truth

Think of all the possible substitute words that might sound more reasonable than 'esteem.' This often turns into an interesting exercise with groups. Self_____?

Very often this exercise generates large lists of alternate definitions for 'esteem.' One word occasionally shows up at the bottom of some lists. It fits the definition of 'maximum value' applied to 'esteem.' What word do you think expresses 'maximum value?'

'Love.' The word that people rarely put on the list. And even when they do, it often seems like an afterthought. Self 'love' qualifies as the best replacement for Self 'esteem.' But, of course, now I have to define the term love.

12

Your Highest Value

So much a victim of our own language, we only have one word in our vocabulary which expresses the emotion of love. The aboriginal natives within the Arctic Circle, I have heard, possess more than thirty different words to describe snow. Supposedly, residents of South America have over 600 different words to define potato. If you live with snow, you need many words to describe different types. If you live among lots of potatoes, you need a great many words to describe them. I understand that certain Middle Eastern cultures have over 20 different words for 'sword,' evolving from a long history of consummate skill in swordsmanship.

At least Latin, the mother of all the Romance Languages, has three different words for love, yet our language struggles along with just one. One! One measly, inadequate word to cover the almost infinite variety of human experience represented by the word 'love.'

Our linguistic limitation results in our saying "I love that music" or "I loved that meal." Little wonder that "I love you," directed at someone we care for very much, sometimes fails to impress. It makes priorities of worth almost impossible to communicate. "I love the music, the meal and you." Not exactly the best message to send to that special someone.

As you probably know by now, love and hate have more in common than they have in dispute. They both focus on one person and express great emotional intensity. That makes it easier to understand why people can so quickly, easily and rapidly shift back and forth between them.

And, of course, love's real opposite shows up as indifference. You can only really convince someone that you don't love them any more if you genuinely no longer care whether they live

An Ultimate Truth

or die. If you express hatred for them, that comes too close to love in its focus and its intensity to carry any weight.

Words such as 'like,' 'enjoy,' 'fondness,' 'appreciate,' etc. represent lesser intensities of emotional value. I suggest that we reserve the word 'love' exclusively for the things in our experience that we value the most: for things that have the most importance to us.

I recommend that we utilize all the other words at our disposal to represent anything less than what we love. Let 'love' define that to which we assign our highest value.

That which we act to retain or acquire meets the definition of 'value.' We perceive reality in degrees of value, from low to high. Some things in our experience have tremendous importance to us, some things have less. I would urge you to use the word 'love' for only those things which have the maximum importance, the maximum value, to you.

Self 'esteem' equals Self 'love.'

Ask a hundred people the meaning of esteem and you'll get a hundred different answers. Ask the same hundred people for a definition of 'love' and you'll probably get two hundred different answers. I offer you one simple answer for each question.

(Self) esteem must translate and transform into (Self) love-ing and (Self) highest value-ing. I know I have constructed a thoroughly weird sentence but you get the point.

Assign your highest value to the word 'love.' Use that specific word to define that which you perceive as most valuable to you. Use lesser words to describe relatively lesser values.

The most valuable thing you know: your life. Your life: that which you value most highly. That which you value most highly: by definition, that which you love.

Before you can say, "I love you" to someone else, you have to have some qualifications. I can't hang out my shingle to practice neurosurgery unless I have the proper credentials, experience and

Your Highest Value

qualifications. I can't say, "I love you" unless I know how to love my Self first. I have to show you that I know how to deliver the goods, love in this case, to my Self before you will believe that I can deliver them to you. If you see that I can't show any love to my Self, you won't believe me at all when I say that I love you. You will know that I lied.

In the same way, you can't say to someone that, "I know how you feel" unless you have truly experienced what they have experienced. They will know that you have lied if you do.

An Ultimate Truth

13

So-called Codependency

Of course, dysfunction makes it virtually impossible to love your own life.

In our dysfunction, we have permission to love other people's lives, no problem there. But, to 'highest value' our own life, never! The inability to love our own life fits the profile of so-called codependency wherein **any** external value has more importance to us than our own value. Other people's opinions matter more than our own; other people's truth appears more accurate and real than our own; other people's happiness seems much more important than ours. External matters, internal doesn't; that defines codependency.

The drowning, codependent person sees someone else's life parade by in front of their eyes, not their own.

If my identity depends upon someone else's evaluation of me, I swim in deep water with hungry sharks and look like bait.

If my emotional state depends upon the people around me, I will quickly learn what a yo-yo feels like. I feel as they feel, when they feel. What they experience, I experience. I behave like a complete emotional parasite. I have no feelings of my own.

Even my thoughts require approval or validation from other people. The idea of having my own opinion about something, and standing up for it, fills me with terror.

These painful realities typify the so called codependent person. Rather than codependent, I prefer the definition 'externally focused.' I believe it more accurately reflects the truth.

'Externally focused' means that everything that matters originates 'out there.' What exists within me has no value, importance or significance. I desperately 'need' others to tell me what to do, feel and think. I completely depend upon others for my identity, mood and opinion.

This 'externally focused' type of dysfunction prevents our real identity from ever emerging. That unique person, withering and dying within us, never gets a chance to see the light of day. We go to our graves with our unactualized Self still trapped inside. What an unspeakable tragedy.

An 'internally focused' life presents a totally different picture; one in which we actually pay attention to what goes on inside ourselves, physically, emotionally, intellectually and spiritually without feeling selfish and guilty about doing it.

In a few more pages, I will show you how to accurately assess your 'internally focused' choices and determine whether or not they deserve the 'selfish' label.

14

Controlling with Guilt

This 'internal focus' sounds like a completely alien concept to anyone raised in a dysfunctional family system.

Such a system can only focus on its primary components, the parents. Only the one(s) within the system who have all the power and control get the attention, directly or indirectly. Everyone else spends most of their time anticipating, fearing, hating, wondering, questioning and reacting to him or her, especially the kids. No one, and especially no child, ever gets to pay any respect or attention to their own reality.

In order to survive, they have to keep their entire sensory apparatus trained upon the main player(s) in their system in order to know what to do or not do, say or not say, feel or not feel, think or not think.

It doesn't take long for a kid to figure out how to gain acceptance in such a system. **For the child, survival means constantly focusing on someone else's state of mind, not their own.**

If we do this throughout our childhood, we will keep doing it as adults. As children, we programmed ourselves for survival and it obviously worked because we still have a life.

Unfortunately we have no way to know that the 'external focus' program in our head exists until it gets us into trouble. Then we don't know how to identify the program, how to understand it or how to rewrite it.

'**Internal** focus' has no chance to develop in a typical, dysfunctional family system. '**External** focus' will emerge as an individual's primary method for dealing with reality.

An Ultimate Truth

When you and I emerged into this world, we behaved the way an 'internally focused' creation needs to behave at birth: with total Self absorption.

Exaggerated egocentricity characterizes every new born child. At that time of our life, the entire universe revolves around us. We can't visualize a reality that does not have us at its center.

Survival of the 'Self': our primary, internal focus at the beginning of our life. The physical, intellectual, emotional and spiritual facets of our Self perform at full capacity to enable us to survive. At this time, we typically experience full functionality. Everything works the way the Designer intended it to work. Since we really want to survive, we put everything we've got into the job of making sure that we do. Whatever it takes, we will do it. We have the capacity to freely and fully devote all of our four aspects to the job at hand.

As long as we get our own needs met, we really don't care much about the needs of anyone else at this stage of our life. Me, me, me! We take on the characteristics of the ideal survival machine. We will make it at any cost. We have no conscience to get in the way at this point, no compassion for others to slow us down, no fear of consequences to limit us and no guilt over past behavior to crush us.

We behave in a way that appears ruthless. We take no prisoners in our battle against anything that could even remotely impede or threaten our survival.

This single minded, fanatical dedication elevates us to the status of kings and queens of our own kingdoms, with everyone else relegated to the position of servants to our exalted states. I believe Freud referred to this stage as 'his majesty the child.'

One of the primary jobs of a parent involves dethroning this beast.

The process of socialization requires the parent to teach the child how to delay gratification and postpone pleasure. The child must experience some frustration and receive instruction regarding

Controlling with Guilt

how to creatively channel that frustration energy into adaptation, postponement and moderation.

One of the most common control tools used by parents involves loading a kid up with guilt. As I said earlier, with regard to parents slapping the 'selfish' label on children in order to control them, "kids behave better when they carry guilt on their back and in their heart. They will frequently not act out on behalf of themselves if they see that Self as undeserving of love and acceptance."

So what can a parent most easily use to drive some guilt into their child? Right, whatever the kid spends the most time doing. Children spend most of their time fully engaged in the job of survival. They spend most of their time 'inner focused.' They spend most of their time using the four facets of their Self to help that very Self survive.

A parent simply has to convince a child that behaving in a 'selfish' or 'inner focused' way will result in a loss of parental approval, love and acceptance.

Since 'inner focused' on the Self virtually defines the young child's constant state, children will see themselves as **constantly undeserving** of their parent's positive regard since they can't suddenly stop doing what has seemed natural for them since birth.

They can't blind their inner focus, they can't turn off their survival switch, they can't quit behaving in a 'selfish' way.

In other words, they find themselves in a real can't/must conflict. They **must** not lose their parents' love and/or acceptance yet they **can't** stop their 'selfish' behavior.

The outcome of this conflict can only result in short term guilt and, eventually, long term shame. Children will experience a profound sense of failure and inadequacy because they feel totally unable to live up to such unrealistic expectations.

The parent has programmed the child to automatically experience guilt as self punishment for 'internally focusing' on the Self. The consciousness of the child has now internalized the concept of 'selfishness.' Every time they 'internally focus' on the Self, they will experience overwhelming guilt.

An accusation of 'selfish' will make the kid do almost anything to remove the stigma of that dreaded label. Now the parent has a mechanism of control, based on guilt, with which they can force the young child to accede to their wishes.

Telling a kid that their behavior might get the 'selfish' label sounds, to the ears of the child, like a threat to withhold parental love and acceptance.

As the very young child grows a little older, parental love and acceptance very quickly comes to represent the primary means and mechanism of survival. Any threat to withhold it poses a threat to their very existence.

Fundamentally, a young child knows that those big people, those parents, hold his or her life in their hands. If the parents stop their feeding, sheltering, clothing, nurturing or protecting, the child will not survive. He or she will die. The child intuitively understands that leaving home to lead an 'independent' life at that age could only happen in a sad and desperate kind of fantasy.

The word concept 'dependent' fully describes the state of a child. Their life 'depends' upon these big parent people.

It seems reasonable that a child would choose to try to keep those people, upon whom its life depends, happy.

Going further, all of us, children or adults, deify those who hold our life in their hands.

We will not choose to picture the surgeon about to plumb our internal depths as having had a brawl with his or her spouse the night before our operation.

We will not visualize the pilot of our plane as having just come off a three day drunk.

The lawyer about to plead for our life can not have a headache or indigestion.

Controlling with Guilt

We do not permit anyone who holds our survival in their grip to exhibit human weakness. We have to see them as infallible. We must see them as godlike. Those who hold our existence hostage can not have feet of clay.

Children see their parents this way: godlike and all knowing. If my parents, who have all knowledge, label me as 'selfish,' then their truth prevails. To keep them happy and protect my **very** dependent existence, I will do whatever it takes to obtain some degree of security from them.

If that means that I have to quit 'inner focusing' and stop paying attention to my Self so much, I'll do it. Survival continues as my primary mission. "If they stop taking care of me, I'll die," so I'd better make sure they approve of me by doing exactly what they want. I will have to make very sure that I try to live up to their expectations, realistic or not.

So, the label of selfishness takes the form of a curse from the gods. The notion that I, as a kid, might get slapped with that horrible label fills me with fear. The idea that I might have exhibited some type of selfish behavior overwhelms me with guilt for having violated the expectations of the god(s).

Then the child grows into an adult, still carrying this terror of a selfish act. Below consciousness, our inner voice constantly reminds us that if we commit a selfish act, we will lose our parent's approval, love and acceptance; quite a burden to bear for all those remaining years of our lives.

We never received instruction as to the rest of the picture. Why would we? Dysfunctional parents found out that guilting us would give them a great deal of control over us, without a lot of work. Educating us with knowledge about the opposite side of selfishness would not have benefited them. They would have lost power and control.

Abuse, by definition, occurs when any parent uses their power and control to violate or deny a child's physical, intellectual, emotional or spiritual boundaries.

An Ultimate Truth

15

Alternative to Selfishness

A flip side of the selfishness coin does in fact exist.

I agree that selfishness, particularly as expressed by us as very young, maniacally egocentric, children does present a destructive, negative, stress inducing, ego-out-of-control scenario.

However, a word concept does exist that expresses the opposite of selfishness in every respect. It presents us with a constructive, positive, stress reducing, ego-under-control alternative.

Before I offer you this word concept, please put something on your inner shelf. Try to recall something you did which absolutely, positively fits your definition of selfishness. In your opinion, you definitely committed a selfish act. You feel guilt even now for having committed such a vile deed. I will soon ask you to pull that event off the shelf and bring it back into focus.

Self interest: the other side of the coin. Self interest: that which adds value to either the quality or the length of your life. Self interest: continually manifesting by virtue of the constructive, positive, stress reducing and ego-under-control choices that you make.

Any choice that you make which adds value to the quality or length of **your** life contributes to your Self interest.

I emphasize the word 'any.'

For example, you had a number of options to choose from this morning when the alarm shattered your slumber. You could have rolled over and grabbed a few more minutes of snoring. You could have chosen to totally ignore it and not get up at all. You could have leapt up from the bed, ready to take on the day. The application of a little imagination could supply a great many interesting options and possibilities.

An Ultimate Truth

The option you did pick represented your decision to choose the one that best satisfied your Self interest **at that time**. Tomorrow morning you may well choose a different option; the morning after that, another.

Most people who have responsibilities rouse themselves and get to work. Why? How does that choice satisfy their Self interest? Well, working will pay the mortgage, put food on the table and clothes on our back: all things in our Self interest.

Most people eat and drink something at the beginning of each day. Why? Perhaps to keep healthy and have enough energy to get through the morning. Sounds like another choice made in our Self interest.

Most people bathe, shower or in some way cleanse themselves hygienically first thing in the morning. Why? Perhaps to avoid disease and avoid offending others: certainly in our Self interest.

When you left your dwelling today, you probably wore **some** type of clothing. Why? Perhaps to avoid imprisonment or keep your Self from freezing to death. Sounds like you made some more Self interested choices.

And all these choices made in your Self interest occurred only this morning. Consider all the other choices you made today, thousands of them; the vast majority of them clearly in your Self interest.

In fact, we always make choices that we believe favor our Self interest **at the time**. Two seconds later we may make an entirely different choice, at **that** time, because we have received new information.

The starving person who robs a store for the money to satisfy their hunger will, if asked, claim that they believed they acted in their Self interest at the time. From their point of view, eating at that time represented their highest personal priority. They had numerous other options to consider, such as: suffer the agony

Alternative to Selfishness

of starvation; borrow some money; earn some money; sell something for cash; burglarize or mug a prosperous victim.

Food certainly represents a starving person's highest current priority. However, the **way** they go about getting it requires making a choice from a large list of options. While eating certainly serves our Self interest, the way we choose to obtain our food may not. Destructive choices result in taking value away from the quality or the length of our life. We satisfy our Self interest when we make constructive choices that benefit us in the greatest number of ways over the greatest length of time.

For example, stealing food briefly satisfies our Self interest. But, if we wind up in jail, The choice has not satisfied our Self interest in the greatest number of ways. It has satisfied it in the **least** number of ways. Gaining a meal at the cost of our liberty results in the **least** amount of time enjoyed satisfying our Self interest, not the most.

Satisfying our Self interest results from making constructive choices.

To reintroduce what I had said earlier: "Constructive choices: those adding value to the quality or length of your life." **"Your 'life' includes those people whom you value. Positive and negative choices apply to you and includes them. That which benefits you also benefits them. That which benefits them also benefits you. You share your existence with them."**

Valuing those you love definitely satisfies your Self interest. Your interest equates with their interest. Treating other people with respect and treating them as you would have them treat you satisfies your Self interest.

Self interest covers a lot of territory.

You serve your best Self interests when you highly value your Life, and the lives of those you love.

Your Self interest requires you to strive to make constructive choices.

Your Self interest requires acknowledgment that, 'I did not completely create myself.'

Above all, your Self interest requires you to take responsibility for your choices.

Now, earlier I asked you to keep an example of an actual, perceived selfish act on your inner shelf in order to bring it forward at my request.

I now make that request. Please drag out that example and take a long, hard look at it in the light of our recent discussion of Self interest.

Does it still seem totally selfish? Does it seem as selfish as it did before we got into the topic of Self interest? Does it look in any way different to you? Consistently over the years, more than ninety five percent of the people I gave this exercise to reported that the example they had chosen no longer appeared genuinely selfish.

On the other hand, some people picked examples from their past so heinous as to contain no redeeming attributes of constructive Self interest whatsoever.

How do you see your example? Does it still appear genuinely selfish? Does it look any different to you?

You may feel pretty good when you realize just how many of your innumerable daily choices serve your constructive Self interest and just how few of those choices truly fit the definition of destructive selfishness.

In our dysfunctional childhood, most of us only received permission to take credit for achievements too big for our parents to ignore. Only the greatest of our accomplishments warranted recognition and celebration.

We typically had no permission to take credit for lesser successes. If we had the temerity to take unauthorized credit for some small achievement, we would inevitably suffer another withering application of the 'selfish' label.

16
Picking and Choosing

I said that your Self interest requires you to take responsibility for your choices. You may think that you can avoid responsibility for your choices by not making any. Not so.

Every choice has consequences. You may prefer to call them results or outcomes. Regardless of how you label it, when you make a choice, some kind of outcome or consequence will result.

Options define that which we pick from. The act of picking out one option from many defines choice. One pick equals one choice. The act of choosing means picking one option from among more than one.

Try to imagine a situation in which you truly have only one option to choose from. "I had no choice!" puts words to it. Assume you have free will and that no one has any control over you.

We usually have many options to choose from, regardless of how undesirable or unthinkable some of them might seem to us. We **have** them, whether we pick them or not.

So, try to imagine a situation where you absolutely, positively believe that you only have one option to choose from, regardless of the quality, desirability or character of that one option.

No such situation exists! We always have at least two options to choose from. The least we have: to do something (one option) or not to do something (second option). The bottom line of options: to live or not to live; to choose life or to choose death.

You can sit or not sit, stand or not stand. You can scream or not scream. You can cry or not cry. You can survive or not survive. You can live or not live.

An Ultimate Truth

We will always have at least two options to choose from. Sometimes we will have two hundred. We will never have less than two.

Granted, some of the available options may not have any appeal whatsoever, at this time. That doesn't eliminate them from the list. We can't deny that they exist simply because we don't like them at this moment. At some other moment, we may start drooling over an option that hours earlier appeared totally unacceptable.

Choosing a job, a relationship or a college for example; all three involve picking one option from a group of more than one.

How many options present themselves to me if I have to pick one college to attend among many; one person to befriend among many; one career among many? It depends upon how many colleges, people and jobs I can put on my list.

Suppose I only know one person in the entire world. I still have at least two options: to pursue a relationship with that one person, or not to pursue a relationship with that one person.

The same with having only one college: I can go or not go: two options.

One available job: work or don't work; two again. Nothing in reality says that you have to **like** all your options. Everything in reality, however, says that you will pick one of them and, whether you like it or not, you will, every time.

Even if you choose to do nothing, you have made a choice. Choosing inaction still meets the number one requirement for a choice; it generates unique consequences. Choose something, choose nothing; different consequences, same process. Results simply depend on **what** we choose.

Choosing to do nothing, choosing inaction, can bring about the most destructive consequences a human can experience.

The most dangerous choice we can make and also the most frequent choice people make: choosing not to choose.

Picking and Choosing

Most dangerous **and** most frequent; it doesn't make much sense, does it?

It has the 'most dangerous' designation because choosing not to choose guarantees that some other person will make our choice for us. That other person may or may not have **our** best interests at heart. They will probably put their own interests first. That other person could take the form of a total stranger, a child or our worst enemy. When we give up the power to choose, the world rushes in to fill the vacuum and make our choice for us.

Giving up the power to choose means that we give up our personal power.

Personal power has two aspects. One, the greater the number of options we have, the greater our personal power. More options equal more power. Fewer options equal less power. Having more options to choose from provides us with a higher probability of a satisfactory outcome.

Two, personal power manifests as the ability to have other people see, hear and recognize us, take us seriously and not look through us or treat us as an invisible object.

Choosing to do 'something' always results in less physical, intellectual, emotional and spiritual risk than choosing to do nothing, even when the 'something' chosen turns into something unexpectedly unpleasant.

Let me give you an example from the real world experience of one of my group rehabilitation clients. Our discussion at the time focused upon this very same topic, the danger of choosing not to choose.

He gave this example. During his recovery from a heavy cross addiction to alcohol and a variety of other drugs, he returned to visit some of his old friends in his old neighborhood. He had the good fortune to have an equal mix of buddies on each side of the fence. One group wanted to go out and hit the bars. The other group wanted to stay home, watch videos and drink soda. Both groups eagerly sought his company. He had two simple options, to go out

An Ultimate Truth

or stay in. He could not bring himself to pick from among those two options or introduce any new options. He decided to turn his back on the process of picking anything and instead chose to do nothing. He chose not to choose. He presented himself to both groups as neutral, as someone who didn't care which way things went. So he voluntarily gave up his personal power, avoided the responsibility of making a choice and refused to accept accountability for his own life. As he told his story, the pain of his experience reached out and grabbed all of us listening. The two groups of his friends found themselves competing for him. One group won and swept him up and out according to their agenda. He had thrown his personal power up into the air, and those people who ultimately picked it up after it landed decided what consequences he would experience. His night out on the town set back his recovery two years and almost cost him his life. He experienced profound pain and suffering because he chose not to choose.

Now I ask you, who does he blame for his pain, the ones who simply picked up the personal power he relinquished, and ran away with it, or the one who gave it up in the first place?

Choosing not to choose also qualifies for the title of 'the most frequent and the most common choice.' Why would something so dangerous seem so popular?

What reason do you think motivates most people **not** to want to fully commit themselves to choosing an option?

Right! Fear. Fear of making a mistake. Fear of picking the wrong option. Fear of the consequences of committing an error. Fear of looking like an idiot if what I pick blows up in my face. Fear of the blame that will descend upon me if my choice results in a disaster for somebody else.

Our old nemesis fear again, the great and powerful motivator.

The fear of making a mistake drives us into the quicksand of choosing not to choose. We think that by not committing ourselves, we achieve protection from our own fallibility.

Picking and Choosing

I would like to offer you rational proof that you can not possibly make a mistake by making a choice; that the fear of making a mistake has no basis in reality.

Every option carries both positive and negative consequences, depending on how we view it. Based upon our evaluation of each option and its consequences, at a particular point in time, we will always pick the one that provides the greatest amount of emotional satisfaction **at the time**. Another moment later, at a different time, we might pick a different option. At **that** time however, the option we pick accurately reflects our current evaluation. We will choose a particular option because we want either its negative or its positive consequence **at the time**. Choosing an option for its negative consequence happens more often than you might think.

I will talk with you more about choosing options with negative consequences later. Can you visualize a situation in which you might choose to experience a negative outcome? Please give it some thought and we'll get back to it.

In any event, we will **always** choose the particular option, among the many available to us at the time, which provides us with the greatest emotional payoff. For example, you cannot commit a truly "Self-less" or altruistic act, even if you donate money anonymously, feed the poor, volunteer your time and services to help destitute people or throw your Self in front of a truck to rescue your child and kill your Self in the process. Every one of those choices represent an option chosen which will provide the greatest emotional payoff to you at a particular moment. It **felt** good to choose to do it at the time. Even if you choose to burn for your beliefs and become a martyr for your cause, you still picked that option because you **felt** good when you did. You chose that particular option because it provided you with the greatest **emotional payoff** at the time.

Regardless of how many options we evaluate, we give every option a brief yet penetrating analysis. The process of evaluation itself takes very little time.

An Ultimate Truth

Now I have a question for you. Regarding each individual option, can we possess **all** the information that exists in the universe pertaining to that option? Of course not. The more research we conduct, the more we will learn; but no amount of study will provide us with 100% of all the available, pertinent knowledge that exists.

Consider the impact of this reality. We can **never** have **every** bit of knowledge which exists regarding **any** option. Therefore, every time we look at one and evaluate it, we will see it incompletely. Some information will not appear. **100% of the time we will see less than 100% of the picture.** We will always experience missing data. Therefore every time we evaluate an option, we run the risk that what we don't know could hurt us. More study and research results in less risk, but never zero risk.

Therefore, we base 100% of our choices on less than complete information.

All our choices, every one of them, carry some degree of risk due to the consequences our ignorance might inflict upon us because of missing information. What we don't know can definitely hurt us!

So, when we make a choice and pick a particular option because we believe it will provide us with the greatest emotional payoff at that time, we will have missed something, every time.

Let's say that you have a pile of options to pick from, you evaluate them and you pick the one that you believe provides the biggest emotional payoff at the time: and it turns into a disaster. What now?

Does this mean that you made a mistake? Definitely not! You gave it the best shot you could, based on what you knew, at that moment. Remember, we always have less than complete information. As I said earlier, the fear of making a mistake has no basis in reality. You can't make a mistake by making a choice and this model proves it.

Picking and Choosing

When our choices occasionally turn into garbage (when, not if), we have two options available to us concerning the way we choose to view the disaster.

One, we can deny it and say it never happened. "I don't make mistakes! Nothing like that could ever happen to me. 'Perfect' describes me." We can completely reject the evidence of our senses. We can completely and totally ignore the consequences of having picked a particular option that turned sour.

If we ignore reality and dive into denial, what will we probably do the next time that same option appears before us? Right. We'll probably pick it again. Why not? My denial says that nothing negative happened the last time I picked it.

You can see this at work in relationships. You pick one partner out of many for the positive outcome you expect. In a little while, you discover something about the person that totally disgusts, repels and alienates you. You bring the relationship to a screeching halt. You realize that you missed a great many insights into the other person's personality.

Deny all the evidence before you and you will pick that same person or type of person again, at some future time. Ignore reality and you will repeat it. When we deny reality, who do we blame when it hurts us?

If someone abuses you but says that they love you while they physically or emotionally beat you, and you deny their actions and stay with them because of their words, your denial of reality will cause you great pain. And, if you do leave an abuser but still deny reality, you will just move on to have many more destructive relationships with other abusers.

Denial can kill you, just as certainly as ignoring a lump can kill you with cancer. Ignoring what happened when you made a particular choice that went sour will doom you to repeat that same choice over and over again in the future. You will remain a perpetual victim of your denial, constantly re-experiencing your pain because you keep making the same destructive choice again and again.

Two, our other option when the choice we make surprises us with a negative result. Can you guess?

Sure, we can choose to learn something from our experience. If we decide to learn something, we can decide not to pick that particular option again. We won't have to repeat our pain over and over in the future.

What exact 'something' can we choose to learn from our experience? Remember, we discussed the impossibility of knowing 100% about any option? Our knowledge of **every** option has something missing from it.

The exact 'something' we can learn will consist of a piece of that information we previously had not known about that option and, had we known it while evaluating our option, **we would never have picked it in the first place.**

If you had known in advance that your new job would lay you off in a month, you would not have chosen it as a career move in the first place.

If you had known that your new house sits on an actively toxic nuclear waste dump, you probably would not have bought it in the first place.

If you had known that the school you chose to attend had incompetent instructors, you would not have chosen to go there in the first place.

If you had known that the partner you picked had unresolved homicidal issues or an undisclosed, Self destructive addiction or a deadly transmittable disease, you probably would not have picked that person in the first place.

Choices that turn out negatively have a lot to teach us if we choose to learn. What almost kills us can teach us the most. Even things that merely annoy us can teach us something. If we choose

Picking and Choosing

denial, we won't learn anything and then we will suffer accordingly.

When you make a choice and it doesn't turn out as you expected, does it mean you made a mistake? No, a mistake would only occur if you chose to deny the results instead of choosing to discover what you missed in the initial evaluation of the option.

And who carries the responsibility for our suffering if we choose to deny reality? Certainly not anyone else. We do.

To summarize responsibility: since we always make choices, we always carry the burden of responsibility. We can't escape it. Choose to do something, choose to do nothing; we still choose and our choosing causes consequences to occur. Either way, *we* make the consequences happen.

An Ultimate Truth

17

Boulders, Rocks and Sand

This has the quality of both good news and bad news. The bad news says that no matter what choice we make, we carry responsibility for the consequences. No escape clauses here; 100% responsibility all the time. This could seem like a heavy load to carry. It means that when we screw something up, **we** screwed it up, no one else did. The consequences flow from us. We can only decide whether we want to deny the reality or learn from it.

The good news says something you've probably never heard before. It says that when your choices generate positive, terrific and wonderful consequences, guess what? You still **must** carry 100% of the responsibility for those results, the same way you must carry it for the negative outcomes.

You carry the obligation to own up to your successes. No humility allowed. If you did it, you must take credit for the positive results, just like the negative ones. We truly carry 100% responsibility for every type of consequence that flows from our choices. If you earned it, you must accept responsibility for the positive results. If you didn't earn it, then obviously you can't take any credit or responsibility for what happened. But if you did, you must.

Mental health results from many things. Balancing our view of reality ranks right up there, near the top. Our dysfunctional family systems of origin usually held us fully accountable for choices that generated negative results. Our responsibility for making choices with negative outcomes counted heavily against us. That same system saw no benefit in forcing us to take credit for those choices of ours that turned out wonderfully. That would have encouraged our 'selfishness.'

For your sanity's sake, you must take credit for both your successes and your failures, 100% of the time.

An Ultimate Truth

I use a simple model with my clients. Visualize a see-saw with an open, empty, metal container nailed upright to each end of the plank. Label one can (+) and label the other can (-).

Imagine that every choice you make during a day entitles you to throw a rock into one of the cans. The intensity of the results determines the size of the rocks. For example, a great big, wonderful positive outcome allows you to throw the biggest rock you can find into the (+) can. You must throw an equally large rock into the (-) can when a choice results in a really terrible outcome. Use decreasingly smaller stones for smaller intensity consequences. Use grains of sand for the really small ones.

The hardest part of this exercise occurs when we try to keep track of **all** our daily choices; not an easy task. Nevertheless, try to log as many as you can.

You have one other requirement. You should try to visualize the sound of these various sized rocks, stones and sand grains rattling and crashing into each can. I have had many clients over the years come into a session proudly announcing that they had "Dropped a boulder" into their (+) can because they took appropriate credit for achieving a significant positive outcome.

Above all, keep track of the small positive outcomes, the grains of sand. They add up. That goes against all your past programming. However, your mental health may one day depend upon this simple procedure. I have seen this model help to save more than one person's life. Don't treat it lightly.

Because of our childhood programming, we get accustomed to keeping track of only our negative results. The idea of keeping track of our positive outcomes seems alien, even disloyal to our family rules. We bear full responsibility for **all** our choices, both positive and negative. We must keep equal score if our mental health and our functionality has any constructive meaning for us. If it has no meaning, we won't. The choice falls totally into your lap.

18

To Bake a Cake, or Not

I hope the message about the crucial importance of your choices came through loud and clear. Let me give you a real life, nuts and bolts example.

Many clients start off a therapeutic relationship by asking someone in the mental health field to show them how to attain greater functionality.

They frequently have tried all sorts of ways already, and have generally failed to find anything that works. They have usually read everything they can get their hands on, for years. They have waffled in and out of therapies. They have tried everything that their friends recommended. They have tried the weird and the traditional. They have attended every course and lecture they can afford. They have tried retreats, escapes and clinics.

The mental health person will often, unofficially, give them a test by providing them with some new information. We need to see what they will do with it.

I compare this to the process of baking a cake. A client says they want the recipe. They say they want to bake a cake. Fine. We provide them the list of ingredients. The moment of truth comes when the client chooses what they want to do with it.

They have at least two options. Sound familiar? To accept the ingredients (option one) or reject them (option two). If they reject them, they clearly have not yet reached the point where a therapeutic relationship has enough perceived value to warrant getting involved.

On the other hand, most people will accept the list of ingredients and then ask for instructions on how to mix everything together in order to apply the ingredients to the process of making

An Ultimate Truth

the cake. We will give them directions. Now what client options present themselves?

Right. Either they will accept the challenge of responsibility, attempt to mix everything together and apply themselves to the job of baking the cake based on the instructions (option one) or they will not (option two).

If they will not, and if they choose option two, they will sit there with the list of ingredients in front of them and, with the instructions on how to mix them fresh in their memory, say, "Show me what to do!"

Their attitude (attitude: a cluster of beliefs around a particular subject) manifests as a choice to do nothing. They want the therapist to bake their cake for them. They want someone else, anyone else, to do their work for them. Above all, they want someone else to take their responsibility away from them so that they can avoid accountability.

They choose inaction. They choose to do nothing. They often choose to manipulate their therapist, or anybody else they can victimize, hoping that he or she will fall into the trap of doing their work for them.

Often they choose to suffer, preferring to have pity rather than respect.

Many people choose despair and destruction. Anyone who chooses to believe that they have lost all their power to build, to create, to survive or to celebrate their life will usually choose to use the final, great power of the willing, voluntary victim, the power to destroy. Those who choose to suffer will attempt to destroy the lives of those who don't, if they can. Those who choose to ignore beauty will try to destroy those who can still see it. Those who choose death rather than life will not rest until they have destroyed as many people who value life as they can.

Do you really want to choose to bake your own cake or do you just want to have someone else bake it for you?

19

Polishing Your Trophy

The fact that people can voluntarily choose to suffer needs some more, in-depth exploration. Earlier I asked you if you could visualize a situation in which you might choose to experience a negative outcome. I asked you to give it some thought. Hopefully you have. Did you have any success?

This makes an excellent topic for a dynamic group discussion.

Why indeed would anyone choose an option with a negative outcome? As I said a few paragraphs ago, they will if they prefer pity to respect.

My wife, Deborah, named the behavior beautifully. She and I had concluded a group training session and she observed that a couple of members seemed to have a lot of pride in their misery, so much so that they refused to even consider letting go of it. She said that it appeared as if they treated their 'problem' like a trophy which required regular polishing in order to achieve notice, due to its brilliance, from other people. They appeared to need to troll a very shiny attention getter to hook an audience. Ever since then, we have used the term 'trophy polishing' to describe an individual's process of making choices which will result in misery in order to manipulate others into feeling sorry for them.

Think of the benefits of holding on to a real 'problem' or a valid 'issue' as opposed to giving them up. You must experience genuine unhappiness or the scam won't work. If you really suffer, what can you easily get from other people without having to work for it?

Their attention; their compassion; their focus on you; their time; their advice; their money; their suggestions; their recommendations; their help; their support; their pity.

An Ultimate Truth

Quite a list of strokes; and you only have to maintain your misery to get every item on it free of charge, with no work and without taking on any responsibility. What a deal.

What would anyone else have to do in order to get the same goodies, without resorting to trophy polishing?

Right! They would have to earn it. They would have to work for it. They would have to stand on their own two feet and take responsibility for their life. They would have to take the risk of making choices and choose to learn from those that blow up in their faces. They would have to choose life instead of death.

In order to earn someone's respect we have to work hard, very hard.

In order to get someone's pity, we don't have to work hard at all; we just have to glue ourselves to our pain.

You can test the waters for trophy polishing. When someone chooses to suffer, suggest some reasonable ways for them to get out of the pain and achieve some kind of relief. Their reaction will tell it all. If they accept the reasonableness of some of your suggestions and agree that what you said makes some sense and if they take some steps to walk out of their pit, they choose in favor of their constructive Self interest. If, however, you receive nothing but resistance and accusations that, "You just don't understand what happened to me," you should wear very dark sunglasses for protection from the glare of their highly polished trophy. They love (highest value) their misery. You don't stand a chance. You will not have any success whatsoever in motivating them to give up on their free ride. If you meet such inappropriate and belligerent resistance, it should look like a red flag waving in your face, warning you of danger ahead. You could easily turn into the person's victim instead of their rescuer.

Many people who have turned into victims of trophy polishers experience a lot of pain. "She keeps me on the phone for hours"; "He needs me so much, I don't know what he would do without me"; "He/she doesn't let me have a life"; "They have

Polishing Your Trophy

nobody else to turn to"; "I feel so sorry for him/her, but their demands on my time drive me crazy." The aggregate unhappiness of the victims often exceeds the misery of the original trophy polisher.

Part of the trophy polisher's strategy requires victims to believe that they stand alone as the polisher's only bulwark against total emotional collapse and that no one else exists who could even remotely take their place. They must convince the victim that they depend completely upon them and therefore the victim must never let them down.

This master-slave relationship has the title of 'controlling through guilt, fear and intimidation.'

I guarantee that if you extricate yourself from the trophy polisher's web, they will have another victim on the hook within a matter of minutes. No truth lies behind the notion that you, and you alone, carry the burden of responsibility for someone else's happiness.

If you choose to believe that you must carry responsibility for someone else's happiness, you will have entered the swamp of 'external focus' and so-called codependency which we have discussed before.

Your life and your happiness depend upon you accepting your responsibility. Someone else's life and their happiness depends upon their acceptance of their responsibilities.

The trophy polisher has as their secondary objective the capture of as many prisoners as possible while pursuing their primary objective of obtaining unearned strokes.

You do not need to consider yourself powerless in the face of the unrelenting demands of a trophy polisher, or anyone else. You have great power: the power to choose. Use it constructively, in your self interest.

An Ultimate Truth

20

Never Powerless

Powerful, powerless: when we experience a dysfunctional childhood, in a destructive and emotionally abusive family system, we might easily look back and see ourselves as powerless because we had no ability to fight the system in our very early years. We believed that we just had to go along with it.

Nothing could fall farther from the truth. At no time does any person, of any age, experience genuine powerlessness while still living. I recognize the potential for controversy in this statement so let me explain.

We, child or adult, often wind up as living victims of the choices of other people. Someone chooses to force us into a prison camp. Our dysfunctional parents make choices, intentionally or unintentionally, that force all kinds of pain upon us. A stranger with a gun can choose to force us to pick life or death. A technician chooses to skip a maintenance procedure and our car crashes.

Other people's choices frequently victimize us, no doubt about it. Sometimes their choices can even kill us. What can those who fail to kill us **not** force upon us?

They cannot force us to see the situation as they want us to see it. We can always choose **how** we want to see it, how we want to deal with it and how we want to react to it. The power to make those choices remains safely in our possession, unreachable by those who would, if they could, turn us into completely powerless victims.

'Powerless' never applies to a living victim. People always retain their power, no matter how excessive or destructive the victimization.

What a victim chooses to do with their power presents another story altogether.

Some people will use their power to survive, create and cope.

This category applies to any child raised in a dysfunctional family environment. That child will direct all their power towards survival. When they choose to go along with their family system and its dysfunctional demands, they choose to do so in order to survive. The concept of 'survival at any cost' drives the child.

All too often the cost involves a deep wounding that leaves a legacy of physical, intellectual, emotional and spiritual scars.

When you or I faced the trauma of dysfunction, we chose to survive, obviously. But at what cost? We never knew that the price of survival would extract so much from us or add so much pain to our reality.

Survival yes, but all too often a survival that bludgeoned us to our knees and then slashed us until permanent emotional gashes remained that will always fester, weep and refuse to heal.

The rules of engagement never stated that we would survive our dysfunctional experience unscathed, standing straight and tall with clear skin, straight teeth and an unbroken spirit; quite the opposite. Sometimes we survive as a helpless, hammered, screaming, bleeding shred of life that only knows the agony of pain upon pain upon pain.

If this sounds unreal and overly dramatic to you, count your blessings.

If this sounds familiar, you have my deepest, most compassionate, sympathy. I've experienced the horror I describe; so have many of my clients. Unfortunately, so have millions of other dysfunctional people.

So, some people will use their power to survive create and cope. Some won't. Those who won't may use their power to achieve completely different, antithetical objectives.

As I said earlier, the power to destroy remains the last great power of any individual. Whether they choose to destroy their own life; the life of another; buildings; personal property or ideas, it still amounts to the use of a great power. The power to destroy has the same intensity as the power to create. It may travel inward, and destroy the individual, or it may travel outward to destroy external people or things.

A dysfunctional childhood environment eliminates the perceived value of a child's own Self. When that child moves from highly valuing its Self, as originally programmed at birth, to rejecting, denying and hating that same Self, the power of the child will shift from survival mode to destruction mode. The kid doesn't suddenly lose his or her power when the shift happens, they just change the direction and the nature of their power.

They go from constructive to destructive; from survival to extermination.

My favorite example involves a fire hose in use. The tremendous water power flowing through the hose usually requires several people to control, aim and direct the flow. You've seen the firefighters struggling with the python-like hose while it whips around trying to get free from their grip. It almost seems alive. When we have healthy, functional beliefs, we have no problem directing the power flow in the direction that best meets our needs and serves our constructive Self interest. All our power can flow in the direction we want it to go, with little effort. We use our power for the benefit of our Self.

When we acquire unhealthy, dysfunctional beliefs about our Self, we turn against it. Now we use our power against the Self. We turn the hose around and blast ourselves with it, aiming for our most vulnerable parts.

We can easily succeed in destroying our Self with the same power we formerly used for our survival.

As long as we still live, the hose flows. Only the direction of the flow changes. Unfortunately, our survival tool can easily turn into our suicide implement. Same tool, same power; different objective, different direction.

An Ultimate Truth

An applicable example involves our choice-making process. When we choose destructive options instead of constructive options, we have turned the fire hose around. The nozzle now points directly at our jugular. What causes us to do that? Beliefs: destructive, dysfunctional beliefs. Where did we get those beliefs? From a dysfunctional childhood family system. Deadly simple.

As I said, powerlessness never applies to a living victim. What we choose to **do** with our power always applies.

How do you direct **your** power? Where does that snaky fire hose point?

Hopefully this all sounds familiar. Choosing life versus choosing non-life, a minute by minute process; exercising your power in favor of one or the other.

21

Deferral, But Not Forever

At this point, discussing choices, power and responsibility usually generates a few questions about procrastination. I have spelled out the manifold dangers of choosing not to choose but procrastination can look like an altogether different animal.

When we choose not to choose **yet**, we have simply picked another of the many options available to us.

I said earlier that we always have at least two options to pick from. We may have many more, but never less than two. Actually we never have less than two options **plus one** to pick from. We could have a thousand options before us and actually we would have one thousand plus one to pick from. That extra option never leaves us.

So what gives with this extra option? Isn't that just what we don't need, another thing to evaluate?

Suppose you have three colleges to pick from. You evaluate each one in terms of the possible consequences that might occur if you pick 'it.' You play 'what if.' What if I pick this one? What consequences will I experience? What if I pick that one? What positive and negative outcomes might occur?

What would happen if you evaluated all three college options and still felt unable to pick one?

Now you can pick the extra option, the 'plus one.' This option carries the label of 'deferral.'

In the case of your three colleges, you may want to gather more information about one or more of them. You may want to talk to some former students or faculty that you have not yet reached. You may simply need some more time to complete your evaluations.

An Ultimate Truth

Then take it. Pick the 'plus one' option. Choose 'deferral.' You will have chosen a totally appropriate thing to do under the circumstances.

However, deferral doesn't mean forever. A deferral must have a time limit. You can defer for a minute, an hour, a day, a week, even a month. But a deferral without a time limit has all the characteristics of a destructive fantasy.

Procrastination, or avoiding responsibility, happens when you choose not to put a time limit on your deferral. An open ended deferral, with no final point in time for accountability, just evolves into irresponsibility.

You could even defer again, once you reach the time limit, if you need to do more research. Perhaps you could even claim another deferral after that one, but you can't do it endlessly. You can't duck a decision by outrunning it. Any attempt to do so turns into a choice not to choose.

Avoiding choices, responsibility and accountability takes a lot of energy. It eats up a lot of our time. We have to work at it. All this avoidance meets the definition of a 'drug of choice.' A drug of choice must distract us from our pain. Anything we choose to put into our body or our mind could wind up as a drug of choice. I emphasize **anything**.

22

The Most Common Drug of Choice

One of the things that my clients often choose to put into their heads does a great job of distracting. In my opinion, it represents the *most* common drug of choice. Creating chaos identifies that drug of choice. Choosing to create chaos, where accountability applies to nobody, really works. Keeping things stirred up makes everything a moving target and hard to hit. It also makes it possible for a controlling person to keep everyone off balance and on the defensive.

If a controlling person can force victims to focus on externals only, in order to keep chaos from overwhelming them, they won't have the time, energy or ability to resist their abuser.

Chaos keeps everybody guessing. Victims have no way to feel sure of anything. Nobody can pin the tail on a moving donkey. Direct questions don't get direct answers, just vague mumbling or no answer at all. Everybody has to guess and, in the absence of clarity, any guess could turn into a disaster. Everyone spends most of their time in fear, waiting for the ax to fall. High anxiety rules this state. With no trustworthy benchmarks or guidelines available, the victims have no way to accurately measure success or failure.

Chaos works really well as a distractive drug of choice. Keeping things fuzzy, fearful, anxious etc. means that no one will have the time or the energy to hold me accountable for anything, a major secondary fringe benefit of indulging in this particular drug.

We have a full time job keeping the waters muddy and making sure we don't have to look at the painful emotions lurking just below the edge of our awareness. The demands of the job preoccupy us and protect us from awareness, just like any other efficacious drug of choice.

I have clients who love to create chaos. They can't keep appointments without making a dozen changes and numerous reschedulings. They will always forget things important to their appointment. They make sure that the causes for the chaos they create always appear external to themselves. No accountability for them. Their emotions can only focus on the fantasy of those supposedly external causes and how unfair or unreasonable they seem. They have no desire to pay attention to their own reality. Distraction at all costs. I personally believe that chaos, as a drug of choice, provides more defenses against insight than any other.

23

The Buried Will Rise Again

I need to present an important model to you at this point. The sequence of events in the model has shown up in every client I have ever worked with. It certainly showed up in my own case, many years ago.

First, childhood dysfunction separates us from our original, functional Self. This separation occurs because as children we must bury anything that gets in the way of obtaining love and acceptance from our parents. Dysfunction begins this way. We bury thoughts and we bury feelings.

We put on the required act and play the part expected of us. We learn to play our roles brilliantly and wind up putting even more distance between our act and our buried thoughts and feelings. Our original, functional Self gets pushed farther and farther into non-awareness.

We start to believe in our own act. We successfully disbelieve, reject and deny our Self because it just gets in our way as we try to rip some love and acceptance out of the tangled fabric of our family system.

Our functional thoughts, feelings and needs can't get met in a dysfunctional system so they hide. They hide in our deepest and darkest inner refuge: that part of our mind below consciousness. They don't die, they hide. They don't lose energy, they gain strength as the years pass. They wait, and they look for opportunities to remind us of their existence.

If you think that all the painful emotions you stuffed into your below conscious mind as a child have disappeared just because you can't remember them, think again.

An Ultimate Truth

They manifest in a thousand ways. Other people pick up on them. Children zero right in on them. Animals react to them, sometimes very strangely.

Your sense that you couldn't bear the shame if anyone **really** knew the truth about you, tells you that they exist. Your deep fear of disapproving voices, looks or attitudes proves it further. That sense of profound isolation and loneliness which occasionally sweeps over you says it all.

Second, the greater the distance separating our acting Self from our whole, real, pure and original Self, the greater the emotional pain. That pain expresses itself in various devastating ways.

Every time we split off, deny or bury a part of our Selves, we bury the emotions attached to that part at that time. When we repress the part, we also repress the emotion connected with it.

For example, when I help clients reclaim a piece of their early life, the emotions released will come directly from that age and that developmental level. The emotions can look, sound, smell, taste and feel very primeval and very powerful indeed.

A brief note: repression differs from suppression. Suppression refers to a very short term denial. It might soon reemerge so that we can deal with it. Then again, it might not. Repression will last a lifetime if we don't get any help.

Even though we have repressed so many of our parts, along with their attached emotions, they still make their presence known to us. For example, we often experience present anger along with the effects of past anger. Present anger occurs when something threatening happens now. If someone cuts us off while driving, our healthy boundaries activate in order to protect us and we feel a totally appropriate degree of anger.

Unhealthy things happen when our old, buried anger sees the present anger as an opportunity to get a free ride up to the surface of our awareness. Remember, I said that those buried emotions wait and look for any chance to remind us of their existence. So, instead of feeling an appropriate amount of Self

The Buried Will Rise Again

protective anger towards the driver who cut us off, we experience enough anger to want to kill him or her; not healthy or appropriate.

Repressed emotions work like that. They wait for opportunities to hook onto something else moving into our awareness and then they emerge full force.

You've experienced it. Something minor occurs and you react to it as you would to something major, totally out of proportion to the situation.

Other people observing you usually ask why you went overboard like that. They can't understand it. You can't understand it. The experience frightens and confuses them. It frightens and confuses you. You have no answers as to why you went so far because of so little. Now you do.

This applies to every other emotion too, not just anger. Grief can suddenly overwhelm us at a time when we have just experienced a slight, fleeting moment of sadness. A reasonable small fear about something can suddenly mushroom and immobilize us with anxiety and panic. Flashbacks can turn a friendly occasion into a life and death struggle. Even laughter can get out of hand and turn into hysteria in the most embarrassing situations and locations.

Repressed emotions can also manifest in another way. We've discussed how they can hook onto emerging emotions and explosively vent to the surface of our consciousness, adding their energy to the energy of our present emotion.

The other way doesn't happen quite so readily or predictably. We can all feel gratitude for that. Many of my clients have described this second type of experience as the most frightening thing they have ever experienced.

Method one required the presence of a real, current, active emotion, which would then act as a host and as a trigger for the repressed emotion.

Method two needs no such carrier. Repressed emotions can strike out of nowhere and leave nothing behind but screaming.

An Ultimate Truth

My clients who looked back at their experience with method two all voiced the same hope: never again, please, never again.

Unfortunately it comes again, and again. It comes when least expected and with no warning. It comes with savage intensity at our weakest moments. It comes whether we like it or not. It shows no mercy and we can't control it.

Overwhelming emotions boiling up out of nowhere; to call this terrifying doesn't even begin to approach accuracy. Raw, blinding, strangling panic might come a little closer.

To make matters worse, we can suffer from both the hook-to-present and the sneak attack at the same time.

So, when I describe the pain of separation from our Self, I want you to understand the nature of that pain and some of the many forms it can take. The emotional pain of this kind of separation can exceed the pain of any other type of human isolation.

It manifests in the deep, tragic realization that the separation actually exists; that we had to separate from our Selves in order to survive in the first place; that because of that split, some of our most visceral thoughts and feelings may remain hidden forever from our own awareness; that we may never again reunite with those missing sweet and gentle parts of our Selves; that our repressed emotions will cause us to suffer for the rest of our lives.

These painful realities can produce excruciating agony, day after day, year after year with out any hope of respite.

They will do it from their secret, protected location beneath our consciousness. Below conscious thoughts, beliefs and feelings can harm us. They can even kill us.

They can fuel our dysfunction for a lifetime, with all the energy it will ever need. What we don't know can hurt us, deeply and profoundly.

The Buried Will Rise Again

And, through it all, we can have complete ignorance of the firestorm of feelings engulfing us as it rages and burns us just below our threshold of perception.

To recap: first, childhood dysfunction separates us from our original, functional Self. Second, the greater the distance separating our acting Self from our whole, real, pure and original Self, the greater the emotional pain. Third, the greater the pain, the greater the need to distract from that pain. More pain equals the need for more distraction. That seems reasonable. When we hurt, it always helps to get our mind off it and on to something else: a common experience for all of us. Certainly we experienced this in our childhood when our parents tried to make us laugh or feel better with the bribe of a new toy or ice cream so that we would stop crying if we fell down and bloodied our Selves.

If only our parents would have allowed us to have our pain and cry like crazy, with their loving approval, until we had satisfied our need to experience and express our grief and/or anger. But no, their efforts usually focused exclusively on getting us to stop experiencing and expressing our real feelings. Typically, our parents' discomfort with their own emotions motivated them to try so hard to get us to stop expressing ours. Often they had a terrible time dealing with their own feelings and felt uncomfortable around the unbridled emotions of children, with their lack of restraint. Our parents' emotional dysfunction transferred to us in the form of repression, denial and fantasy and we will inevitably transfer that legacy on to our children if we don't choose to make the process come to a halt within ourselves.

Think of the times you had fear as a kid: real, gut wrenching fear about something. What did you hear? "Oh you really shouldn't worry about going to the dentist. Only sissies fear that old drill. Nothing should cause you to make such a great big fuss. You didn't really have a bad dream. You make such big deals out of nothing. Don't cry, only babies cry."

Repression, denial and fantasy substitution. All first order distractions; some of our earliest programming, designed to swing

An Ultimate Truth

our attention away from our negative experience and hook it on to some other, less painful object. Anything would do, as long as it did the job of distracting us. Eating disorders started if we swung over to food. 'Stop crying, eat this.' So when we felt bad, we learned that we had to eat something. Since life often gives us reasons to feel bad, we eat a lot. Soon someone weighs 400 pounds and wonders why.

Worry makes for terrific distractions. Once we get caught up in the hamster wheel of worry, we can't get out. Worry drowns out all previous concerns. It works as long as we keep worrying. If we stop, all the old haunting returns. We learn to see worry as preventive medicine.

Ingesting chemicals of any kind provides a massive range of distractions from pain. Over working, over exercising, over gambling, over sexing, over anything that clouds our original hurt and creates the fantasy that it no longer exists will do. Fantasy over reality. In reality I hurt, I really hurt. In my fantasy, no more pain. Some new sufferings perhaps, but at least not the original anguish. The original terror can seem to have reduced itself to a constant but manageable ache. Of course that constant, manageable ache also registers as a daily reminder of the original beast and as such, it must have its own distraction. Distraction piles upon distraction. The layers get deeper and deeper. Pretty soon we have almost lost conscious sight of our original pain but the accumulated effect of all our distractions can create a totally new kind of horrific specter to torment us.

At this point, clients often ask me to distinguish between obsessive/compulsive behavior and addictions. I'll give you the brief answer. First of all, obsessive refers to the activity of our conscious thoughts. If we obsess on something, we can't stop thinking about it. Compulsivity refers to things we do. If we wash our hands fifty times a day or count the tiles on the kitchen wall every time we sit down to eat, that demonstrates compulsive behavior. Obsessive/compulsive behavior distracts us from our pain with rituals. If we stop obsessing or compulsing, we feel great anxiety because we fear the return of the pain. Obsessive/compulsive behavior relieves pain because it distracts us from its return. **Addictive** behavior provides powerful, emotional, mood altering pleasure as the mechanism of distraction.

I also get questions about the difference between impulsive and spontaneous. Impulsive involves *doing* something. Spontaneous means *feeling* something.

The objective of any distraction has at its core the driving desire to change the way we feel about our original pain. We must alter our feelings. I prefer the word 'emotions' to the word 'feelings'; a matter of personal preference on my part. Another synonym for feelings, the word 'mood' often shows up, as in 'mood altering.' Like the word 'attitude' which, as I mentioned earlier, means a group of beliefs about a particular subject, mood refers to a group of different emotions revolving around a central theme or topic. 'Mood altering' really means 'emotions altering' but since mood altering rolls off the tongue so much more easily, I will use it. Distraction requires mood altering.

The greater the pain, the greater the need for distractions. The greater the need for distractions, the greater the need to mood alter. The greater the need to mood alter, the greater the need for a drug of choice.

We discussed drugs of choice before. Anything can serve as a drug of choice and I mean anything. As long as we put enough of it into our body or into our mind, it can do the job.

We can have physical, intellectual, emotional and spiritual drugs of choice. Usually we need to mood alter in more than one of our four categories, since the original pain affects all of them in varying degrees. If anything we choose consistently and effectively changes the way we feel about our crummy relationship with our Self, it meets the definition of a mood altering drug of choice.

An Ultimate Truth

24

Your Priority Relationship

Clients often ask me if I would work with them and their partner to salvage their relationship. The relationship that they want healed has a much lower priority than the one that really matters. The relationship that REALLY matters of course involves your relationship with that original Self now lying buried under the rubble of the years of your repression, denial and fantasies. Join the Club. Unfortunately you have a lot of company.

If we can bring our relationship with our Selves back to a functional level, our relationships with other people will exactly reflect that increased degree of functionality and improve proportionately. We will start showing up on the radar screens of healthy, functional people that we never knew existed. It takes some time to happen, but it always does.

Do not ask why your partner behaves in such a destructive way towards you or why he or she abuses you. If by some miracle someone could tell you exactly 'why,' what would change? Nothing! Your partner would still beat you and humiliate you. Your knowledge as to exactly why they do it won't take away one bruise or scar. Your understanding of **them** won't help you understand **you**. You have to understand why **you** stay in a destructive relationship, not why the other person behaves the way they do.

When we start the process of genuine recovery, our existing, previously established relationships will tend to travel in one of three possible directions.

First, our friend or partner might see us getting help, and really recovering, and want a piece of what we have. They might start asking questions about our new, more constructive process of thinking and feeling. They might ask to get similarly involved. We might inspire them to take action in their own self interest. If we could do it, why not them?

An Ultimate Truth

Second, that person might see the gap widening between them and us; and to prevent it from getting any wider, they could try to drag us back down to their present level, and our former level, of misery. Threats often fly around at this juncture, particularly the threat to leave us if we don't give up our quest.

Third, they might just leave, unable to limit us or handle the changes in us. They can't bear comparison with someone who at one time functioned at their exact level and then chose to stop suffering. The contrast worsens their pain. They can no longer lessen their suffering by sharing it with another victim. Misery really does love company.

I have seen many long term relationships end because only one of the partners got healthier. If both participants in any personal relationship don't share similar goals, they can't continue as a significant, meaningful partnership. Friends maybe, but no longer intimate partners. Often this type of relationship switches over into a business arrangement of convenience rather than a shared celebration of life.

Many people have these businesslike arrangements masquerading as an intimate relationship. To many dysfunctional people, a business deal sounds a lot better than no deal at all. The fear of isolation causes a lot of people to make some very accommodating arrangements, with guaranteed fantasies and distractions but very little joy and celebration. As a result, the emotional impact of living a lie makes vacant, empty eyes stare back at us from the mirror. It shreds the heart and makes sadness our companion in the shadows. It brings despair home to stay.

I often get questions about the nature of a healthy relationship as opposed to an unhealthy one. I have a single word answer: sharing. Sharing everything defines a healthy relationship; not just sharing a few selected things but a 100% sharing. **Sharing doesn't necessarily mean agreeing, but it does mean full disclosure.** Unhealthy relationships revolve around secrets and hiding.

A healthy relationship has mutual, Self-interested choices at its core. An unhealthy relationship will sink in the swamp of

Your Priority Relationship

Self-ish choices. Selfish choices, by their very definition, preclude sharing and full disclosure. They do not permit an awareness of other than Self.

If two people join together out of mutual neediness alone, their relationship will self destruct. However, if they come together as two independent people who have learned how to functionally get their own needs met and who then want to share all of their experiences with each other, they have a good shot at survival.

If two people both 'need' each other in order to find happiness, satisfaction and joy, neither one of them can give. Two needy people can get enmeshed and locked into an embrace of mutual misery, with nothing to offer the other. "I need and I want; fill me and complete me!" This desperate, needy supplication can't find fulfillment or satisfaction from another needy person. How could it? We want what the other person can't give us. They don't have it to give. We don't have it to give either. We definitely want it, but we can't give it or get it.

I can 'need' to share my life with another; I can 'need' to 'highly value' another and love them; I can 'need' to receive the love of another; but if I 'need' another person to make me happy, codependency has me by the throat. A joining based on neediness won't work. Neediness means that someone other than my Self carries the responsibility for my happiness. Only a relationship based on each of us carrying the full responsibility for our Selves, getting our own needs met and then sharing our joys and sadness, failures and achievements with another will have a chance.

An Ultimate Truth

25

Explaining The Attraction

All too often, we get trapped in a cage with someone who, by every reasonable standard, can only cause us harm. We've all seen this: people who have nothing between them but hatred, violence, rage, victimization and misery. Any acquaintance who knows either one of them always asks the same question, "How can you stay with him/her?"

Obviously something catches us in its paralyzing grip and holds us there. That 'something' has to have so much appeal that we choose to risk our lives to gain whatever it offers by way of a payoff.

Usually the answer to the question, "how can you stay...?" sounds like this: "I know that things don't look too good between us some of the time, but when things go well, I feel terrific!" The payoff surfaces. Hard drug users say exactly the same thing. "I may have to lie, cheat, steal, rob, kill, or sell my children but when I get high, I feel so terrific that I forget all about that stuff."

Both 'highs' share the characteristics of an addiction. In an addiction, we voluntarily choose to have a destructive relationship with anything that has life threatening, or quality of life threatening, consequences. We initially chose not to say no and then once we have a few super high, mood altering experiences under our belt, we can't say no. We can't imagine our life without that payoff experience.

Obviously in chemical addictions, changes occur in our body chemistry which make it impossible for us to voluntarily choose to stop by an act of will alone. Our body just won't let our conscious mind successfully get us to quit. Our altered **physical** state now biologically requires the presence of the drug in order to function and our body uses our emotions to motivate us and drive us to get more of it.

An Ultimate Truth

In non-chemical drugs of choice, the mind rather than the body uses the emotions as a motivator. Our altered **mental** state now requires the presence of the non-chemical drug to function and uses our emotions to motivate us and drive us to get more of it.

Our altered, dysfunctional, mental state drives us to stay in a destructive relationship to get those few rare, but deeply satisfying, payoff experiences. Our emotions force us to get more of it, not less. We feel terrible when we don't have it and terrific when we do. We will tolerate almost anything in a relationship to get those elusive, mood altering highs.

Those highs can't come to us from any other source either; no substitutions allowed on this menu. Only a certain type of relationship can provide the kick: a destructive one. It has to give us the rush of a near death experience, constantly, either as a victim or an abuser. So we stay in it. We stay in it until it kills us or we kill it. Either we will choose to remain a victim of the relationship or the relationship will end up a victim of our choice to survive.

26

Onward to the Flame

So what do we want so badly that we risk life, limb and sanity for the experience?

We need to satisfy our desire for something that doesn't exist elsewhere. If it did exist elsewhere, we sure would have gone there first, not into the suffering of a destructive liaison.

We need to feel an emotion: a particular emotion; a unique emotional experience that we can't find anywhere else. That specific emotion, or group of related emotions, that we yearn for points directly to something we missed in our early life.

Let me give you an oversimplified but factually accurate example from my client files. Two mature, physically healthy people, a male and a female, suffered the pain of a destructive, long term relationship from which neither could extricate themselves. What they shared with each other met all the criteria for an addictive union. Mostly it caused them both considerable pain, yet both said that the good times made it all worthwhile.

During the long weeks between their mood altering payoffs, they each entered the therapeutic process with me, separately. Their backgrounds had very little in common, with one exception. They both had childhood relationships with the parent of the opposite gender that forbade open expression of any emotion, especially anger; he with his mother, she with her father. They both had entered their maturity with an unmet need to express anger.

Both of these people had a history of rejecting suitors who treated them respectfully and with kindness. If nothing in a relationship made them angry, if everything went well, each of these clients couldn't run away fast enough. Their friends who saw them reject one decent, caring person after another labeled them strange.

An Ultimate Truth

When these same friends saw the two clients locking up with each other, after writing off so many other more apparently desirable partners, they labeled them very strange. When they saw them flaming in and out of their love/hate ritual, they labeled them crazy. When they saw them suffering together for years and still aggressively defending the enmeshed relationship that neither one of them could end, they labeled them hopeless and dangerous.

Their friends got very nervous. So did their families. They each had children from previous, destructive relationships. Those kids got real nervous.

So, what do you think? What drove these two intelligent people to not only fly into the flame like moths but choose to stay there, slowly burning?

They both really needed to express present anger and a whole lot of past, buried anger. They both desperately needed an outlet. They both needed a reason to feel anger, a reason that made sense. Separately they both made the same statement about the other, "He/she makes me feel so mad!" There lies the key. Each one needed the other to make them mad so that they could each have a guilt free, sane, valid reason to yell, scream and holler. They needed to feel justified before they could throw a tantrum, behave hysterically, scream, kick things or hit something. Those choices had to have the sanction of and the permission from a good reason. They gave each other that good reason, they gave each other the permission they needed to express their anger. They needed to continue as collaborators to make it possible. Congenial people who treated them nicely had no value whatsoever in their scheme of things. They required an alliance with someone who could really get under their skin. They needed a caustic irritant.

Repressed emotions, looking for a way out, can make strange bedfellows. Repressed emotions never die. They just wait, and find ways to remind us of their existence.

This example described only one particular way in which our repressed emotions can force us to find an outlet. Everyone has a different set of unmet emotional needs bubbling in their basement, sending out tendrils to touch the emotions that motivate them every minute of every day.

Those buried emotions want to get our attention. They demand their freedom. They want us to disperse their pent up energy. They refuse to lie quietly while we march to the grave with them in bondage. We can ignore them but they won't go away. Somehow they'll get our attention.

They might even get our attention by causing heart attacks, ulcers, skin problems, impotence, hypertension, anxiety attacks or clinical depression. One way or the other, they will make their presence known.

An Ultimate Truth

27

Your First Survival Tool

Moving from our discussion of repressed emotions, let's dig a little deeper into emotions themselves.

We only have two tools of survival. Each living creature starts its life with unique tools designed to enable it to survive. Other creatures than ourselves have instincts, claws, great strength, wings, teeth, and every conceivable type of specialized survival equipment.

With what unique survival tools do humans start out in life? I said we have two. What comes to your mind?

Other creatures posses greater strength, sharper fangs, better sight and superior hearing than we do. What special qualities enable us to make it?

One of our tools makes us angry, depressed, joyful and fearful, although usually not all at once. Our first tool of survival consists of our emotions. We will discuss the other tool later.

Have you ever thought of your emotions as survival tools? Of all the billions and billions of people who have ever lived and died up to this moment, every one of them, and us, came into this world with a full set of functioning emotions. It takes a while for them to eventually succumb to dysfunction. Emotions seem part of the universal human package. Everybody has them when they come through the door. The Designer must have had a reason to provide them to 100% of its human creations. Clearly they exist for a significant reason, not as some luxuriant frill or unnecessary extra baggage. Their universal nature suggests a universal necessity. Nothing speaks more loudly of necessity than the requirements of personal survival. We need our emotions in order to survive. Let me tell you why.

An Ultimate Truth

Let's take the four main compass points of emotion: anger to the north, sadness and grief to the east, joy and celebration to the south and fear to the west. This simple model includes every human emotion: at these points or in combinations between them.

I will take each of the four emotional points and show you its survival necessity. I will show you how you would lose part of your ability to protect, develop or celebrate your life should you lose the capacity to experience that particular emotion.

28

Why We Need Anger

First, anger. Visualize your life without any anger. By anger, I refer to the full spectrum of anger, ranging from slight annoyance to furious, out of control rage. All emotions always manifest in degrees. Remember that. If you had no anger available to you, you would not have the ability to feel the slightest displeasure or the least little bit of hostility, to say nothing of your inability to get really mad about anything. Consider what your life would feel like without **any** degree of anger available to you. What could you **not** do?

You could not protect yourself. You could not enforce your physical, intellectual, emotional or spiritual boundaries. You could not say "NO!" to anything dangerous. You would have inadequate or non-existent boundaries.

The whole world could stomp up one side of you and down the other without resistance. You would turn into the absolute victim. Anybody could do anything to you and get away with it. Why not? Nothing could make you angry enough to say no, to say 'stop it!' You would have all the survivability of a sheep halfway into the slaughterhouse. Nothing could get through your indifference. No anger means no boundaries.

Anger motivates. Degrees of anger motivate either a little or a lot. From a survival point of view, no anger means no motivation to fight back or protect the Self. No motivation to protect the Self means a very much reduced likelihood of survival.

Having no available degrees of anger results in traveling through life without boundaries. Consider the reality of that. Anything or anyone can get to you at any time, whether you like it or not. You have no power to stop them. No anger means no power.

If a stranger bumps into you on the street and causes you pain, within a few seconds you will find out why. If accidental, you

An Ultimate Truth

will hear apologies. If intentional, belligerent or uncaring, you'll hear that too. You will learn what motivated the bumping. Your emotional response will have a lot to do with their explanation as to why they reeled into you.

But what about your emotional response at the instant of painful contact? Within a few seconds, you will know what to feel about the person based upon their spoken words or further actions.

At the instant of contact however, an emotionally healthy person will feel a brief, fleeting moment of intense anger because of the violation of their physical boundaries. Even if we know and love the person who stepped on our toe, if they caused us pain, we would still feel that quick flash of resentment and anger.

Observe your Self closely the next time something like this occurs and watch your Self experience the sudden hot flash of survival-generated, boundary-protecting anger that grabs at your gut.

Your own emotions will dramatically demonstrate the presence of healthy, appropriate anger as a survival tool.

You can also enhance your boundaries with what I call the 1,2,3 pattern.

With regard to what other people do, anything can happen once. A one time occurrence has no major significance.

If you see it happen again however, you see a pattern in the process of forming.

If you **let** it happen a third time, you have chosen to let the pattern victimize you.

If you get abuse once from your partner, of any kind, it might only happen once. If you get abuse from your partner a second time, you see a pattern in the process of forming. **If you allow your partner to abuse you a third time, you have chosen to allow the pattern to victimize you.**

29

The Safe Haven

I have had many clients moan about having too much anger. They say that their 'temper' gets them into trouble. I agree, it does. Inappropriate degrees of **any** emotion hurts us and others. Isolating ourselves at either end of emotional spectra means that we miss out on the other 98% of what we could experience. When we only function at emotional extremes, just like black and white, all or nothing thinking, it gets us into a whole lot of trouble.

Our functional goal: to experience legitimate emotions appropriate to the situation. We need to match our emotional responses to the reality of the moment, not to the fantasies in our head preceding that moment. Our dysfunction manifests itself in chronic over-feeling or under-feeling.

Dysfunction has the effect of causing us to always see ourselves as something better or worse than human. We can't see ourselves as a balanced, functional entity, possessing both positive and negative qualities. We can only see ourselves as too good or too bad. Our emotions reflect this with either too much or too little intensity. We over react or under react and never find a comfortable center.

Living a balanced, functional life does not mean having a pale, anemic kind of existence. Without the equalization of strong forces, destruction always results. The act of balancing powerful, opposing forces in order to enjoy stability has nothing in common with mediocrity or weakness. On the contrary, it demonstrates great strength and power.

As we shoot from one end of the emotional seesaw to the other, we pass right through the middle and never see it as a place to rest. We develop a sad, despairing belief that such a place can't exist in our reality. We eventually lose any hope of finding a warm,

An Ultimate Truth

dry, safe, 'high ground' to stand upon, where we can catch our breath and bind our wounds before returning to the battle.

I assure you that no matter how elusive the idea of a safe haven seems to you now, it already exists within you.

Please don't misinterpret this statement as something mystical. In no way do I refer to anything irrational, which, by definition, would require you to suspend your reasoned judgment or depend upon faith to make it palatable.

The simple, rational truth states that you started out in life fully functional. We have already established that. The fact that dysfunction may have snagged you with its barbed hooks doesn't automatically mean that you have lost your 'high ground.' No evidence suggests that. Your 'high ground' lies buried and hidden from your view, much like repressed emotions. You and I can clear away a lot of the debris and once again make the hidden visible.

I often point out to my clients and students that legitimate recovery can have all the characteristics of an uplifting, **inward** journey. We can remove the roadblocks as we go and begin to clearly see a previously shrouded reality. This metaphor sounds much healthier than the more common one which says that recovery can only occur through exogenous mechanisms dedicated exclusively to doing, achieving and accomplishing things that have their origins **outside** of our Selves.

I recommend that we replace this codependent, externally oriented thinking with the little acronym PAL. **Permit, Allow, Let**; in other words, let's get out of our own way and permit that 'high ground' which still has life within us to emerge and see the daylight of reality.

If you really want to feel your heart leap, allow your Self to see what a clear view of reality, warts and all, feels, smells and tastes like. Make an effort to move aside some of your garbage and let your Self get a whiff of freedom.

See if you can remember the original functionality of your life as a very young child. Try to recall how you felt when all four

The Safe Haven

of your aspects worked: when you constantly lived in the safe haven of your 'high ground,' before dysfunction dragged you into the slime of the swamp of destructive beliefs.

You really did come into this world on 'high ground.' At that time, you spontaneously celebrated a vibrant, functional life. As you got older, you got separated from your 'high ground' by your dysfunction. Your 'high ground' really does still exist, deeply buried within you.

When we search for our 'high ground,' we peer into our Selves through the muck of our despair. Naturally we can't see it. That doesn't mean it doesn't exist. It just means that we can't see it through the haze of our dysfunction.

At the start of our lives, our fully functional 'high ground' experience gave us a spiritual (spiritual: connectedness to something greater than our Selves) link to that which created our Selves and all the other high, dry and safe newborn Creations. Then, we all still enjoyed the common bond of an unlimited capacity to celebrate our own existence.

As we gradually lost our 'high ground' to the rising tide of dysfunction, we also gradually lost our spiritual link to that which created us. As we lost that connection, we began to experience the misery of spiritual separation and isolation.

An Ultimate Truth

30

Saying Good-Bye

Now, as regards the emotions located to the east on our compass chart: sadness, grief and despair.

How in the world could grief and sadness enable us to survive? How could the absence of the ability to experience grief and sadness hurt us? How could a failure to cry prevent us from weathering the storms of life?

Just as I asked you to visualize the absence of any anger in your life, try to imagine what it would feel like if you couldn't find any sadness to tap. Great, you say, no more tears.

True, no more tears. Can you think of anything you might want to cry about? Can you imagine any situation in which it might benefit you to cry? Can you conceive of situations where grieving and mourning might perform a useful function?

Our whole life moves from one loss to another. We lose our childhood innocence; we lose our naiveté; we lose relationships; we lose security; we lose places to live; we lose parents; we lose opportunities; we lose jobs; we lose happiness; we lose children; we lose partners; we lose people we love; we lose health; we lose people we need. I'll stop now.

We have to constantly deal with some kind of loss. Saying good-bye keeps us pretty busy. Some good-byes don't exactly tear us up. Flushing a dead gold fish doesn't seem too traumatic for an adult. It sure can devastate the little kid who lost it though. That child will cry. We might or might not shed a tear over his or her pain. Each individual suffers their losses in their own unique way. Very young children can't get too worked up emotionally at adult funerals. Adults can, and do. You've seen it. Little kids yawn, while a grieving adult tries to throw themselves into the open grave to follow the one they loved too much to live without.

An Ultimate Truth

We all have very different perspectives on sadness, yet a common denominator, at any age, binds us together. What do you think? What shared experience do we all have as we say our good-byes and shed our tears? How can the process of vigorously expressing our misery help us to survive? How do I have the temerity to characterize anguish as a survival tool?

Grief makes it possible for us to do one very important thing: it makes it possible for us to end something, really end it. Grief and sadness enables us to truly bury the dead and walk away, even though we will stagger for a while.

Without the ability to feel all the pain we can possibly feel about our loss, we can't complete the experience. If we can't complete the experience, we will carry the weight of it, for the rest of our lives, as a constant burden. It will always sit heavily on our shoulders, cutting and chafing at our flesh. It will remain unfinished business, weighing us down or, like an anchor, drag us backward when we want to go forward. We can't recover from the trauma of past losses until we fully experience how much those losses really hurt us.

Shortcuts won't work. Intellectually acknowledging a loss won't have any effect on the emotional devastation we feel deep inside. Those emotions must get out or they will suffer the fate of repression. Then, as repressed emotions, they will leap up and bite us when and where we least expect it or destroy a part of our physical Self as they simmer and fester within us.

It does no good to merely say that, "I feel so bad because my dear friend has gone from my life." It does a lot of good if we yell, scream, cry and feel terrible about our loss for a few days or weeks. Better to vent on purpose than not to and hope the repressed emotions go away. They won't.

Our human design requires us to fully experience appropriate emotions at the time they occur, all of them. Not to experience them disables our survival mechanism.

Saying Good-Bye

Think of all the losses of your life. Go all the way back to your earliest childhood, as far back as you can remember. Try to recall everything you ever lost that mattered. The losses you can remember, with a stab of pain at their recollection, represent those which, for whatever reason, you could not feel bad enough about at the time. At the time of the loss, you could not grieve the loss sufficiently. You did not fully grieve that which reality had ripped away from you, leaving you bleeding at the point of separation.

That wound of separation has to have a chance to heal or it will bleed you to death. Feeling, at last, all the pain of the original wounding, so long buried, can finally close the ragged edges of the gash and allow real healing, real recovery to occur.

Even then, after a full recovery and a total healing, a scar will always remain to remind us of the past. That scar will itch on those rainy days of the heart.

But an itch and a reminder will not have the power to prevent us from surviving. We can survive with our scars.

We can't survive with our open wounds shedding our blood. We must choose to either shed tears or shed blood, one or the other. Shedding tears can finish the pain of our losses. Shedding our blood will finish our ability to survive.

An Ultimate Truth

31

Celebration

The southern point of our emotional compass aims at joy and celebration, happiness and satisfaction. Why must we have full access to these particular emotions in order to survive?

Once again, visualize your life without any of these emotions in it. Pretty bleak, you say? I agree.

Remember the three jobs of a created entity: to protect, to develop and to celebrate its one and only life in this reality. To celebrate: one of the top jobs for a human. What if you felt you had nothing whatsoever to celebrate; that nothing in your experience warranted gratitude or joy?

As dysfunction increases, our ability to spontaneously or intentionally celebrate **anything** decreases. The notion of gratitude gradually loses meaning. The concept of celebration only elicits a reaction of cynical disdain.

Not only do we estrange ourselves, in our dysfunction, from celebrating little things, day to day, we cut ourselves off from celebrating the very fact of our life. Not only do we choose not to keep track of our constructive choices and fill the plus cans on our seesaws but we lose the pleasure of enjoying the ongoing wonderment of our own consciousness and our own existence.

The **un**availability of the emotions of joy and celebration means that we have no emotions motivating us to live or to do that which survival requires. If it doesn't feel good to value my own life, good enough to fight for it, I certainly won't protect it.

A twist to this picture shows up in certain people who only have a partial, limited and selective ability to celebrate and feel joy. These people fundamentally have very little emotional motivation to live but they do have a small crack in their indifference. Their emotionally parched and arid lives will occasionally allow for a

An Ultimate Truth

brief and very intense foray into the realm of pleasurable experience. And how do they get this very intense, 'high,' experience? You bet. They get it from a dramatically mood altering drug of choice specific to their dysfunction. These people spend most of their lives in a vegetative state, but they will occasionally come out of hiding to reach for the emotional stars. Of course this reaching out for something to celebrate requires them to intellectually, emotionally, spiritually or physically consume large quantities of their particular drug(s) of choice.

So the pattern of too much or too little feeling reasserts itself again, resulting in destructive, all or nothing, black or white emotional states, with no shades of gray in between. Individuals either can't celebrate their life at all or they escape into a mood altered state filled with frantic, hysterical euphoria. They can only experience pinnacle or pit. They have no middle ground to rest upon.

32

Fear

Now to the west of our compass: fear. Visualize your life with no fear. See yourself without the ability to feel the slightest moment of holding back, of thinking twice before plunging in. You have no trepidation. If you want to do something, you just do it. You don't bother to waste any time evaluating it first. You equate caution with cowardice.

When you start to cross a busy street, you don't bother to look both ways before stepping off the curb. You have no fear, why should you?

If you get sick, you just shrug off the symptoms. You have no fear of disease.

Perhaps you use steroids to enhance your athletic ability. You have no fear of side effects since you believe that when you get old enough to need treatment, new medicines will save you.

You have no fear of a little bit of white powder. Other people warn you off but you have no fear. You'll snort it, smoke it, inhale it, inject it, eat it or drink it without any fear of consequences. You fear no consequences. You have no fear.

I surveyed a great many cross addicted group participants over the years in rehabilitation programs. Consistently, over 85% of them led early lives which proved that they saw themselves as bulletproof and immortal. They set themselves against huge risks and survived. Sometimes they survived with wounds but the wounds took on the nature of battle scars and sources of pride.

When they came up against hard drugs, they had no fear either. Why should they? Nothing else had ever touched them before, why now? Their past successes had inspired them to have no fear in the present. So they fearlessly tried the drugs, and many of them died fearfully.

An Ultimate Truth

Any drug of choice can make us feel fearless, not just the chemicals that we can put into our bodies. Having no fear at all can kill us pretty quickly.

How long do you think we would have lasted as a child without some healthy, limiting fears?

Without some, none of us would have survived long enough to begin school. We would have crossed one street too many without looking, ignored that one warning about playing with matches or purposely skated on thin ice. Something we ignored, something we wouldn't fear, would have done us in.

The absence of a healthy emotion of fear limits our ability to survive by removing caution, analysis and a desire to evaluate our options before making choices.

Healthy, reasonable fears help us to protect, develop and celebrate our existence, not end it. Plenty of dangerous things exist in the world that we **should** fear, because they could hurt us very badly, or destroy us. Fear will motivate us to avoid, or develop a way to cope with, those things hazardous to our health.

Unhealthy fear plays the game of all or nothing with our emotions. Either we fear nothing or we fear everything. We experience the constant terror of dreading reality or the heady fantasy of invulnerability. Healthy fears can't register in our consciousness when we function at all-or-nothing extremes. An all black or an all white emotional intensity leaves no room for reasonable fears, of reasonable intensity, to squeeze into our awareness.

Since emotions always exist in degrees of intensity, any degree of healthy fear that we can't access reduces our ability to survive by exactly that same degree. We can't benefit from insights that can't reach our awareness.

Interestingly, fear often turns into anger because of the fact that we had the fear in the first place. It angers us that we had the fear.

33

Your Second Survival Tool

What about the second tool of survival? If our emotions form half of our survival kit, what makes up the other half?

The two aspects of the Self that suffer so much from dysfunction: emotions and intellect. We have discussed emotions, now we will discuss intellect, specifically our ability to reason.

We must discuss it, since our ability to reason sets us apart from all other creatures and qualifies as our other survival tool. If we lacked the ability to reason, we would not survive as humans: animals maybe, but not as anything human.

Humans need all kinds of things in order to survive: food, clothing, shelter etc.. How do we get those things that we need? As children, we depend upon parents for them. As adults, we have to get them for ourselves. How do we get them? By what means do we achieve the satisfaction of our needs? With what mechanism do we pursue that which we must have in order to survive?

We act. We take action. We chase down what we need. We make choices designed to get us what we need.

We can't get our needs met by choosing to do nothing and waiting for food, clothing and shelter to magically fall into our lap. If we sit and do nothing, fantasizing about a mystical entity that will come and feed us, we'll starve to death.

Our faith in fantasy won't fill an empty stomach or clothe us or build a dwelling for us. Other people might take pity on us and choose to meet our needs for us, but the fantasy, in itself, has no power to satisfy our reality.

So, we have to hustle in order to get what we need in order to survive. Children feel hunger, period. They don't know how to satisfy that hunger themselves. They have to rely on someone else to find food for them. Parents provide the food for the kid. Parents have to know how to get it. Parents have to choose to act in order to bring home the bacon. Parents have to know either how to grow and harvest the food themselves, and choose to do it, or know where to go to barter for the food from someone else who knows how to grow it and harvest it, and chooses to do it.

The process of survival requires choosing to act in our Self interest. If we choose not to act, we choose not to survive. The things we need to survive do not sit and wait for us, ready made, in reality. They require creation and production. We have to act in order to create and produce them. We can't wish them into existence.

In order to go about meeting our needs, we have to have some facts and some knowledge to start with: about who, what, why, where, when and how.

Then we need some ideas. Ideas, or concepts, integrate our past experience with the present and enable us to plan ahead to make productive choices that will meet our survival requirements.

Creating concepts requires that we use a special type of thought process: reason.

Reason enables us to make what our senses tell us intelligible. Without reason, all our incoming sensory data would seem like gibberish. Without reason, we could only react emotionally to our surroundings, like a newborn baby. Reason allows us to separate, identify and label the flood of incoming sensory information. It allows us to tie-in our present experience with past experiences. It integrates our intellectual knowledge with our emotions.

Reason makes it possible for us to create concepts out of raw, sensory information. For example, sensory data says platform, off the floor, supports, color, texture, length, width, height etc. and reason enables us to form the concept, "table." Reason perceives the facts of reality in the first place; it makes connections between them; it creates symbols to represent abstractions; it arranges and assigns places for more new, incoming information to go; it defines and labels what we have decided to call everything;

Your Second Survival Tool

it sets the stage so that we can see everything clearly, put everything together and go on to form conclusions. Thanks to our ability to reason, we can say because of *this*, then *that*.

Survival means that we have to find or produce that which we need to survive. Finding and producing requires reason, the only effective mechanism we have of dealing constructively with reality, so that we can choose the actions that will keep us alive rather than those which will kill us.

An Ultimate Truth

34

Alternatives Only In Theory

At this point, I often get questions about means of survival other than reason. Let's look at some of them.

Intuition: past knowledge or experience in our below-conscious mind applied to the present which occasionally generates valuable conclusions. Intuition does not acquire new knowledge, it finds new applications for old knowledge, usually in ways our conscious mind failed to come up with. We have no direct control over the intuitive process nor do we have any evidence that we can absolutely count on it coming to our assistance, when we need it or, for that matter, ever. Those who choose to live their lives 'intuitively' have simply chosen not to choose in order to avoid accountability and responsibility.

Accident: the notion that we can survive just by stumbling over pre-formed, ready-made conclusions and concepts that have somehow appeared by magic, waiting and ready for us to fall over.

Revelation: insights from a mystical source providing us with all the concepts and conclusions we will ever need to survive. Again, ready-made so that we don't have to do any work ourselves.

Default: by choosing not to act in our Self interest, we somehow activate an unidentified source of ideas and conclusions that will automatically provide us with what we need to survive.

Luck: an accidental process with a twist; the added feature that, if we win some cosmic lottery, something might just act in our favor and do all our work for us, activated purely on the basis of random chance.

Some people can and do rely on some of these methods in order to survive. They don't survive well. They exist in misery, pain, frustration and despair.

An Ultimate Truth

The way they attempt to go about achieving their delusion requires the introduction of phrases like, "Transcending reason" or "Evolving past reason."

In their mythology, our ability to reason must appear optional and, more importantly, it must appear as only one of many steps leading to some kind of enlightened state. If reason only makes up one step of a path, then we can easily hop over it.

The survival tool of our ability to reason can remain locked in our tool box forever. It can even see some use and then get tossed back in the box by people choosing to deny it in favor of 'alternatives' to reason. The alternatives themselves always wind up as variations upon the themes of intuition, accident, revelation, default or luck.

Reason works. It makes it possible for us to survive. Reason takes a certain amount of hard work to implement. We can choose to suspend our reason. We can avoid the hard work. Dysfunctional beliefs can tell us that mystical short cuts will allow us to live without having to work at the business of survival. These same dysfunctional beliefs can tell us that we have a magical ability to get our needs met, that we can get fed, clothed, nurtured and sheltered without having to get off our tails and create, produce or acquire whatever we need. Unfortunately, mystical short cuts only reduce the length and diminish the quality of our life. They short cut us to an early physical, intellectual, emotional or spiritual death.

35

Free Will

The concept of free will refers, among other things, to an individual's power to choose whether to live on purpose or live accidentally.

Incidentally, the concept of freedom always expresses either "freedom to . . . " or "freedom from . . . ."

To live on purpose means to choose to think. To live accidentally means to choose not to think. To choose to think means to voluntarily use our ability to reason as we activate our conscious mind.

Conscious thinking can occur either with, or without, reason. With reason results in survival. Without reason results in chaos, victimization, pain, suffering and death. We have the 'free will' to choose one or the other.

Living 'on purpose' means making conscious, constructive choices in our Self interest.

Living 'accidentally' means choosing not to choose, choosing not to think, ignoring our ability to reason, relying solely on our emotions for direction (if it feels good, do it) and giving up our primary adult survival tool. We just let life happen to us and around us. Whatever we experience, we experience by accident.

Emotions make up the other half of our survival kit, as we discussed earlier, but as an adult, our ability to reason takes precedence. Reason can make room for emotions and yet still retain the ability to make constructive choices in our Self interest. Emotions can't make room for reason nor can they enable us to consistently make constructive choices in our Self interest. Reason alone remains our primary survival tool.

As very young children we had no ability to reason. Physiologically, our brain doesn't develop the capacity to reason until around age seven or eight. You can't 'reason' with a child below that age level. You would only waste your time and the child's.

Living on purpose means choosing to maintain a conscious awareness of our thought process that matches the reality that surrounds us. Our senses constantly dump all kinds of data into our head and we choose what to do with it. We can choose to use our ability to reason and make some useful sense of it or we can choose to leave it scrambled. If we leave it scrambled, we essentially choose to do nothing and will suffer the appropriate consequences.

So many of my clients suffer terribly from choosing to leave the incoming sensory data in their heads scrambled. What they see, hear, smell, taste or touch remains largely unprocessed, unintegrated and untouched by reason. The cause of their affliction lies in their past reality, as revealed to them through those same senses. Their past had so much pain in it that they just don't want any more awareness. For them, awareness hurts. It feels better not to attempt to put things together in their head. To do so would necessitate seeing clearly what the senses have brought into their mind, both past and present, and they can't bear to directly experience that much agony.

Confronting and defusing the painful emotions of the past makes it possible to rationally face the realities of the present. I'll show you how as we travel further along together.

Intellectual dysfunction: the inability or the unwillingness to use our capacity to reason.

36

Summary

I would like to summarize all we have discussed so far. That would seem reasonable to me, hopefully it will seem reasonable to you as well.

Our Self consists of physical, intellectual, emotional and spiritual aspects.

Functionality means that all those four parts work. Dysfunction means that some, or all, of those parts don't work as intended: for our benefit and our survival.

I did not create myself, something bigger than me had to involve itself in the process of making me. As a created entity, created by something, I have the responsibility to protect, develop and celebrate this life that I received. If I don't, I won't have it for long.

As a created entity, I have awareness of my two primary characteristics: existence and consciousness. I exist and I have conscious awareness of my existence.

My continued existence depends upon the conscious use of two survival tools: reason and emotions. Dysfunction can cause me to ignore my awareness, my survival tools, my responsibilities as a created entity and life itself.

I have the power of my own life and death in my own hands. Dysfunction tips the scales towards death.

Dysfunction came upon me, I did not enter the world with it. If I want to, I can rewrite the destructive programming of my past and if I work hard enough I can do it.

PART TWO

37

Beliefs Reflect Our Truth

I want to quote myself from the very beginning of our discussion.

"One fact has beaten me over the head with its certainty, year after year, with client after client. Every breathing human walking around has a list in their heads that calls all the shots. That list represents and comprises a belief system.

A few "core" beliefs in this system control thousands of "action beliefs." Action beliefs generate 100% of our choices. Our choices generate 100% of our voluntary actions. Our beliefs give rise to virtually all our emotions. They also determine whether we will perceive stress as a positive or a negative experience. I will share a lot more about this with you later.

Your list, and the beliefs engraved upon it, directs all your actions, activates almost all of your emotions and determines the type of stress you will experience. I think that makes those beliefs vitally important and yet most people have no idea what their own list, their own belief system looks like."

I said earlier that, " I will share a lot more about this with you later." 'Later' has arrived. We must dive deeply into the subject of beliefs. Our beliefs rule us. They initiate every voluntary choice we make and virtually every emotion we experience. They determine whether or not we will find reality stressful. They run the show.

Dysfunctional beliefs make our choices destructive and our emotions dangerous. I indicated earlier that the most powerful belief on our list deals with "the most important thing we know." Dysfunction makes us believe that we can never see the Self as the most important thing we know; anything else, fine, but never the Self.

An Ultimate Truth

Once we enter the world, beliefs form fast and furious. Beliefs about what? Beliefs about everything.

Beliefs express our own definition of truth. What we see as true, we believe. Beliefs express our truth. Keep this statement in front of you at all times, please. **Your beliefs express your truth.**

Beliefs form in our brain. They develop as a consequence of the cognitive mental process of a child: the process that determines what we know and how we know it.

Our senses send messages to our conscious brain. Our reason, developed or undeveloped, sorts through it and tries to understand it. Children under seven or eight have no trouble drawing conclusions, even though their ability to reason has not yet fully developed. The small part of our ability to reason that understands cause and effect and makes it possible to say 'because of this, that,' works just fine in very young kids.

The infant learns very quickly that because it cries, it gets fed, or changed, or rocked etc.. What belief has formed as a result of this conclusion? What truth has established itself in the mind of the child? Because of 'a', 'b'. "Because I cry, I get taken care of. That looks like truth to me. Therefore, I believe the truth that if I cry, I will get taken care of. I have a belief."

If, as an infant, I see a parent's face before me every time I get taken care of, I will probably form another belief based upon the apparent truth that equates the parent with care. I believe the truth that when I see my parent's face, I will get cared for. I have another belief.

And so it goes. Tens, hundreds, thousands of little beliefs, all of them based on rational conclusions arrived at within a child's mind.

Every one of our first beliefs revolved around us. Our I-dentity evolved out of our first collection of beliefs about our Selves. That means that those beliefs go back farther than any other beliefs we have. Who and what we see as our unique, personal reality had its origins in the early months of our existence.

Beliefs Reflect Our Truth

Whatever we choose to accept as truth turns into a belief. If I accept a fantasy as truth, that will also turn into a belief.

We did that all the time as kids. We believed in our fantasies, absolutely. Our stuffed animals talked, our big, empty boxes protected us from monsters better than any castle, our tea parties served royalty and our costumes turned us in to anybody our imagination could picture.

Childhood made no distinction between fantasy based beliefs and reality based beliefs. We believed all kinds of perceived and imagined truths equally, side by side. We had no reason to discriminate between fantasy and reality.

Our parents had the job of pointing out the difference to us as we got older. If they didn't or couldn't do their job **then**, we will see no reason to separate reality from fantasy **now**. In a child, that inability to separate reality from fantasy seems cute. In an adult, it defines a debilitating dysfunction.

As humans, we need fantasy. Without fantasy we would have no hope, no imagination, no dreams, no vision, no goals or aspirations; we would have no capacity to look ahead and picture alternatives or improvements. To visualize anything requires the ability to fantasize about something that differs from our reality.

A healthy, functional person will have a huge capacity for fantasy and they will exercise it often and well. That same individual can step completely out of a voluntary fantasy and make a clean reentry into reality. They know the difference between the two states of mind.

A dysfunctional person can't do that.

The ability to clearly distinguish between fantasy and reality, along with the ability to move back and forth between them, does not belong to a person suffering from dysfunction. They can't fully appreciate or occupy either state and usually can't tell which one they inhabit at any given moment. Fantasy or reality seem equally viable. Any boundary separating them barely exists.

An Ultimate Truth

As children we had no need to separate them. As adults, we must if we intend to survive with any of our four aspects still intact.

Truth can rest in reality or float in fantasy. Regardless of the origins of their truths, people will develop beliefs to express them. This applies equally to children or to adults. Everyone, of any age, develops their beliefs around their apparent truths.

A good example of a belief based upon an apparent, fantasy truth occurs in the mind of a child when parents divorce. Young children will invariably blame themselves for the break up. They see that fantasy as truth. They see themselves totally responsible for, and as the original cause of, the divorce, despite both parents' rigorous assurances to the contrary. Truth to that child does not come from reality, it comes from a fantasy. They persist in seeing their fantasy truth as gospel. Then they base their belief on that fantasy truth. Their belief would sound something like, "I believe that mom and dad got a divorce because of me." The child's persistence in maintaining that belief in the face of a contrary reality probably reflects the presence of other perceived fantasy truths such as, "My worthlessness drove them apart," or, "If I had acted more like the child they really wanted, this would never have happened," or, "I didn't measure up to their expectations and my failure caused their unhappiness with each other." If these other perceived fantasy truths also existed, beliefs would form around them. All these beliefs could easily add up to a certainty that they alone had caused the parents to divorce.

We humans form our beliefs to express our perceived truths, at any age. Perceived truth can originate in reality or it can originate in fantasy. Once a belief forms, it doesn't matter where the underlying truth originally came from, the belief sets in concrete.

Beliefs once set serve as the basis for all of our choices, all of our voluntary actions, virtually all of our emotions and most of our stressors.

Intellectual dysfunction results, more than anything, from creating beliefs based on fantasy truths.

38

Opinions, Beliefs and Convictions

Our first beliefs focused on us. Our earliest beliefs defined our Selves and began the establishment of our I-dentity. As time passed, the magisterial, egocentric child had to eventually acknowledge other subjects in its realm. Other people gradually required some acknowledgment, especially when some of those other people fed, clothed and bathed us. Necessity forced an awareness of other entities upon us.

So then we started to develop beliefs about other people and about our relationships with those other people.

As we got a little older, we eventually saw hints of a world beyond me and thee. It slowly registered on us that more stuff existed 'out there' than under our noses. The more we learned about 'out there,' the more we had to develop new beliefs about what our senses dumped into our heads.

The sequence of belief acquisition matters a lot. First, beliefs about me; then beliefs about you and me; then beliefs about you, me and them.

The beliefs about me go back the greatest distance. The others don't go back quite so far.

Since dysfunction invariably has its roots in our past beliefs, we often have to dig up those first and oldest beliefs since they have great power derived from years of repetition and reinforcement.

Beliefs don't spring forth fully formed, no matter what our age. They start out as mere opinions. An opinion represents a **new** belief that has not yet established itself with any appreciable degree of certainty. Opinions don't have great weight, moment or energy. Opinions need great flexibility in order to change and accommo-

An Ultimate Truth

date new insights and new information. Opinions must alter and transform as our senses provide us with data we didn't have before.

Opinions that remain unchanged for long periods of time can take on the characteristics of a belief. We will consistently act on a belief since it expresses a deeper truth. A belief has a lot of weight and significance. Beliefs have a lot more power than opinions.

Beliefs that remain unchanged for long periods of time can take on the characteristics of a conviction. Convictions have the most power. Due to years of repetition and reinforcement, they carry great weight. They have received validation through frequency.

Old, deeply held beliefs, that have served as the basis for our choices over many years, achieve the status of convictions. All our earliest beliefs about our Selves meet the definition of convictions. They have the most power. They influence more of our choices, actions and emotions than any others.

Incidentally, affirmations won't work. Simply repeating mantra-like words or phrases that you have nailed to your refrigerator, your forehead or to the dashboard of your car won't change anything. It will feed your fantasies, but it will change nothing in your reality. Running words through your consciousness in the hope that, by some magical process, they will transmute into convictions amounts to the worst kind of destructive fantasy. **Only by acting on new beliefs can we make them ours.** Merely repeating words in our heads does not qualify as the kind of action that works. It only qualifies as another manifestation of our destructive fantasies.

39

Core Belief Number One

I need to take you back to some of the things I said to you in the very first pages of this book. Consider it a refresher in one sense and the completion of a circle of information in another.

"I would like to ask you to identify just one core belief from your own list. I'll make it easy for you. I will ask you a specific question in order to lead you towards that particular belief on your own, unique list.

Question: of all the realities that you could imagine or experience, which one, above all the others, seems the most important to you? Which one would you fight to retain? Which one would you refuse to relinquish?

"In other words, what exists for you as the most important thing your senses can perceive?"

"At this point, I usually reformat the question as a statement. Name the one thing without which all the other important things would seem meaningless to you. If you don't have it, you couldn't have any of the other things of relatively lesser importance."

"What ever you have chosen for your answer identifies your most significant core belief, affecting more of your choices, emotions and actions than any other belief on your list."

Your most significant core belief expresses what you see as truth regarding the topic of 'the most important thing you know.' Whatever holds the title of 'most important thing' for you represents your perceived truth and, of course, your belief expresses your truth. If you believe that you, your life, your existence meets your definition of 'most valuable thing,' then you have a

An Ultimate Truth

very healthy and reality based core belief. If you have a core belief that says you believe that anything else occupies that position, I can only say, "Welcome to the world of major dysfunction!"

Let me further reintroduce you to more of what I said in those same, earlier pages.

"YOU, YOUR LIFE, YOUR EXISTENCE identifies the most important thing you know. Without your life, within which you perceive all the other important things, you would have no ability whatsoever to appreciate and prioritize anything else that you see as valuable, worthwhile or significant. You have **got** to have **it** first.

If your answer named your partner, how could you express your high regard, love and value for him/her if you did not first exist? The same applies to your children or your grandchildren. If you value and love them, you can't show that love to them if you do not exist. You can't protect that which you value without first manifesting your own presence.

You've got to have your own life first. All the rest comes second in priority. Even if you want to sacrifice your life for somebody else, you have to possess that life in the first place before you can give it away. Sacrifice requires you to exchange a higher value (you) for another, relatively lesser value (the other). Exchanging a lower value for a higher value doesn't fit the proper definition of sacrifice. It fits the definition of a good deal and a bargain. That which you perceive as worthy of the highest value you can assign to anything defines **you**.

Spirituality, a sense of connectedness to something greater than ourselves, becomes impossible without the existence of your life necessarily preceding your awareness of that connection.

You: the most important, valuable entity within your awareness! Your life, the most valuable thing you know!"

I can't reach out from these pages and grab you by the nose to get your attention. If I could figure out a way to do it, I would. Maybe a 'pop up' page design would work. As you open up this

Core Belief Number One

particular page, my paper fingers could hook you by your nostrils and force you to focus on these words.

I would ask you, as my Client, about your most important core belief. I would listen very carefully to your answer and probably ask you a lot more questions. Since I can't do that, the total responsibility for asking your Self questions falls on your shoulders.

If your core belief does not express the truth that you see your own existence as the most valuable thing you know, what do you see as most important?

For the moment, I have to leave you in your own hands. If you have any interest whatsoever in breaking free from dysfunction, you must start here. You must answer that question about your primary core belief. In your heart of hearts, in your deepest, most private thoughts, what do you see as your 'most valuable thing?'

An Ultimate Truth

40

Our Earliest Programming

What happens when you have a belief? How do your beliefs determine 100% of your choices, 100% of your voluntary actions, a little less than 100% of your emotions and almost all of your psychological stress?

Where does a belief get so much power?

From us. Humans empower their own beliefs by acting on them, over and over again. We choose our beliefs the same way, and by the same mechanism, that we make any other choice.

I will quote myself again.

"Every option carries both positive and negative consequences depending on how we view it. Based upon our evaluation of each option and its consequences, at a particular point in time, we will always pick the one that provides the greatest amount of emotional satisfaction **at the time**. Another moment later, at a different time, we might pick a different option. At **that** time however, the option we pick accurately reflects our current evaluation. We will choose a particular option because we want either its negative or its positive consequence **at the time**. Choosing an option for its negative consequence happens more often than you might think."

We choose our beliefs from among two or more options, just like we would in any other reality based situation. How does this work when we pick core beliefs as very little children? How do we handle the options we perceive at that age?

Studies have placed hundreds of young children in exactly the same environment and conducted exactly the same tests on every member of the group. They generally get hundreds of different responses to their tests, Why?

An Ultimate Truth

Philosophically, everyone seems to feel comfortable with the observation that, "Everybody sees things differently."

We do all see things differently, at any age. We all bring a totally different window with us, at birth, through which we view reality.

Our scope of current knowledge says that while we, as infants, bring a blank *conscious* slate with us, our below conscious mind comes preprogrammed with some information already in place through the mechanism of our genetic structure.

Current wisdom estimates that about 20% of who and what we will become already comes with us as part of the package at our birth. The 80% balance of our destiny lies in the hands of our physical, intellectual, emotional and spiritual environment.

The genes we came with had already loaded some predispositions into our mind before we came on the scene; some of them constructive, some of them destructive; some of them healthy, some of them unhealthy.

Every one of the cells in our developing body had the same genetic coding packed into it so that every cell would know where it has to go relative to every other cell. Our genes programmed the nature and placement of every one of the trillions of cells that make up a total human body.

Every cell in our brain has that same genetic pre-coding; so does every cell in every other internal system that influences our thoughts. It doesn't take a lot of imagination to see that if a newborn child has external, physical features similar to those of its parents, and also some other physical characteristics from relatives in generations long past, it will also have some internal, mental characteristics similar to its predecessors as well. You've heard it. You may have even said it. "That child has its mother's eyes, its father's ears and its great grandfather's temper."

The gene pool that we tap goes back a lot farther than just a few generations. No one really has a handle yet on just how far back our common genetic material does go. You can read the

Our Earliest Programming

scientific journals just as well as I can. Some sources draw connections to ancestors many, many thousands of years in the past.

I want to make sure that you, as you read this, keep in mind that the genetic material that makes up our body also makes up our brain and our other mind related systems. The cells that make up our brain determine how we think, what we think about, how we process incoming sensory data, how we form our intellectual connections, abstractions and conclusions as well as our emotional responses.

Heredity genetically pre-establishes about one fifth of our temperament, intelligence, learning ability, speech, motor skills and every other activity involving a mental process.

So we, even as infants, already have some fairly extensive programming in place when we first look at options in our reality.

That programming helps determine which option among many we will choose, even at that early stage of our development. In addition, our own, self initiated programming quickly starts to impact our reality through the application of our emerging beliefs and the conclusions drawn from our ever increasing experience. Our experience educates us.

As we get older, educational systems, both formal and informal, will also start to add to our experiential education. If systematic education failed to do its job for just one generation, the next generation would have to start all over again, from the very beginning of knowledge. They would have to reinvent the wheel. Genes only transmit individual physical and mental characteristics from one person to another. Genes can't transfer the knowledge of a culture, a philosophy or wisdom from one generation to the next. Only continuous, uninterrupted education can do that.

An Ultimate Truth

41

Unpredictable Outcomes

To summarize, once we perceive two or more options in our head we will either pick one, defer till a later time in order to gather more information or choose not to choose.

Once we perceive two or more options in our head, and if we decide to go ahead and pick one of them, three things will motivate us: our desire for the greatest emotional payoff at that particular moment, our genetic preprogramming and our conclusions derived from previous experiences.

No sane person would attempt to predict what would emerge from this process. For example, in the mind of an infant, at any given point in time, the number of possible outcomes becomes a very, very big number and they only have preprogramming and emotional payoffs motivating them. For an older child, not to mention an adult, the number becomes astronomical, because for people older than infants, experiences enter the equation and add even more variables.

So we have no way in reality to predict what will come out of the process of picking options We can only deal with the results of the process **after** the fact.

If the results of the process, after the fact, become destructive to the individual or to others, we can try to get the person to change some of the variables that went into their particular, process. We can attempt to get them to look critically at all three of their inputs: the nature of their emotional payoffs, their predispositions and their previous conclusions from other experiences. The therapeutic process demands a lot from both client and coach. It takes a lot of work. As yet, no one has found any rational shortcuts.

An Ultimate Truth

42

Evaluation Defined

We must go further into the choice making process to understand how our beliefs drive it.

As we view the options before us, in our head, we evaluate each one of them, briefly and deeply, in terms of positive and negative consequences. We play 'what if I pick that one."

I need to address the concept of 'evaluation.' What does it mean to evaluate something? What actually goes on in our minds when we evaluate anything? What do we really do when we evaluate?

Let me give you a simple yet effective example that I have used many times. Picture a defendant before a judge: no jury in this example, just the defendant, a court reporter and the judge. The reporter reads off the charges against the defendant; the judge hears them. The judge has to 'evaluate' the information and reach a decision. Did the defendant break the law or not? What goes on in the judge's head? Before a judgment can occur, an evaluation of the information has to take place. What does the judge do with the information just received concerning the actions of the defendant? Can the judge make a decision based on intuition, prejudice, bias or mystical insight? Possibly, but it would never hold up on appeal. What must the judge do with the information that he or she received about the defendant in order to meet the requirements of the justice system?

The judge must compare it. Compare it to what?

You know what every law office has in abundance: books. Law books, stacked from floor to ceiling, going back for years, citing thousands of previous cases and giving interpretations of statutes. Books that contain the actual statutes take up shelf after shelf. The library holds all the information that defines the law itself. The law itself, in all its endless interpretations, represents the

An Ultimate Truth

standard for measuring people's choice-making behavior. The statutes name the rules and the cases show the details of enforcement over time.

Now, I'll ask you, to what does the judge compare the defendant's behavior? Right, to the law itself. The judge can't compare the behavior to his or her own personal opinion, that would result in disbarment. The judge compares the behavior of the defendant to the law, or laws, that govern such types of behavior. Guilt or innocence depends upon the outcome of that comparison.

Evaluation equals comparison. When we evaluate anything, we make a comparison. We compare what our senses tell us with something we already have in our head that we use as a standard of measurement. Any ideas as to the identity of that standard of measurement? Sure, you see the logical answer: our beliefs. Full circle; home again. We compare incoming sensory data with our beliefs to determine the nature of what we perceive, according to our particular, unique belief system.

I have a simple illustration to make the point. You, me and one other person sit in an empty room. We each have different beliefs about spiders. You don't care one way or the other, as long as a spider doesn't try to harm you. You believe in live and let live. I, on the other hand, get really worried if spaghetti looks like eight legs. Spiders terrify me. I see them as the spawn of dark forces. I believe that they hate me and want to hurt me. I suffer from spider paranoia. The third person in the room had spiders as childhood companions and loves them.

To justify this silly story, as it happens, the biggest, hairiest, spider ever seen by humans suddenly crawls into the room. You yawn. As long as it doesn't menace you, you remain safely wrapped in your indifference. I, on the other hand, have already left the building in my desperate sprint to freedom. The third person hugs the spider and gives it a name.

Now for the obvious question. Did the spider cause the three different reactions? Absolutely not. The spider acted as an

Evaluation Defined

activating event. The spider just showed up on its way to the web. Our different beliefs caused our different behaviors. We each evaluated the spider by comparing our sensory input with our own beliefs about spiders and each of us reacted in complete accord with our own beliefs. **We always react emotionally in complete accord with our beliefs, 100% of the time.**

When we evaluate our options, we compare what our senses tell us, about each option, with the beliefs we already hold. Based on that comparison, we will pick the option that best satisfies those beliefs. By satisfying those beliefs, we provide ourselves with an emotional payoff. In doing so, we reinforce the validity of our beliefs. Since those beliefs provided us with a satisfying emotional payoff at the time, we will act on them again and again in the future. By acting on beliefs over and over, we turn them into convictions.

Our beliefs enable us to define what our senses bring to us. As we evaluate options and compare what our senses tell us about those options with our beliefs, we define and develop a view of reality that we will act on. If our beliefs express functional, constructive, reality based truths, our actions will lead us to protect, develop and celebrate our lives. If our beliefs express dysfunctional, destructive, fantasy based truths, we will act to diminish, demean and destroy our lives. Our beliefs determine our evaluations; our evaluations determine our choices; our choices determine our actions. Therefore, **our beliefs determine our actions**.

An Ultimate Truth

43

Pre-language

Our beliefs do, in fact, determine our actions because beliefs determine our choices. In the process of cause and effect, beliefs determine evaluations; evaluations determine which options we choose; option-choices determine our actions or inactions and, therefore, beliefs cause our actions.

So what.

If beliefs cause our actions, then our actions give evidence of our beliefs. Simple and logical. What we choose to do, or not do, displays our beliefs to the world.

If you saw complete strangers go out of their way to try to kick cats, what evidence would their actions give you? Would you have evidence that they highly valued cats? Only if they valued them as dog food. Their actions would give you evidence of their beliefs, about cats. Obviously they believe that they should do away with cats, which reveals a deeper belief that, probably, cats should not exist. How did you reach your conclusion about the strangers believing that cats should not exist? By observation. Observation of what? Their actions. **Actions reveal beliefs!**

Actually, the fact that actions reveal beliefs came to all of us as experiential truth very early in our childhood development.

Consider this: for a child, language doesn't even begin to develop as a **primary** learning tool until around eighteen to twenty four months of age. At the two year point, a child enters the "preoperational" stage wherein he or she can understand simple questions and name their own body parts. Before they reach that point in their development, however, they have to learn how to actually use a language; how to activate their physical speech mechanism; how to build a vocabulary and how to apply their cognitive abilities to both making and understanding sounds. They experience the first two years of their lives without the benefit of understanding a structured, formal, complex language that could help them comprehend and interpret their environment or their experiences.

Certainly we associated environmental sounds with external objects or internal feelings from the very beginning of life. Those associations, and any verbalizations that represented those associations, did not constitute a use of or an understanding of a complex, structured, formal language. They constituted a primitive, concrete, simple and unstructured language incapable of expressing abstractions. We may have said our first word at around one year of age and, in so doing, put an end to our pre-linguistic stage, but we didn't start stringing both abstract and concrete concepts together into meaningful sentences, intelligible to ourselves and others, until we had a couple of years of life under our belts; child prodigies who hum crossword puzzles, talk in complete paragraphs during their first year and get their Ph.D.'s at twelve notwithstanding.

We start out at birth with a dry sponge for a mind. Dry, not as in 'not wet' but dry as in having lain in the sand, under a blazing inferno of a sun, on a scorching, searing, baking desert for a thousand cloudless years. That kind of dry.

And from the moment of our birth, every single bit of information that our senses feed into our head falls like a drop of water onto that sponge.

We inhale new information just as ferociously as we took in our first breath. All the input from our senses falls like a monsoon rain upon that parched sponge of our mind. During those first two years, even though we can't fully understand the complex, structured language of older people, we take in more information for the first time than we ever will again. Once our understanding of what others say to us begins to improve, we add a new dimension to our ability to comprehend and interpret what our senses tell us about our reality. **But, we will build upon what has already soaked into our sponge, up to that point in our development.**

Pre-language

During our first two years, prior to learning how to use and comprehend formal language, whatever we experience will set the stage for the play we will act in for the rest of our lives. Our roles will start to develop their scripts. The eighty percent of our programming not predetermined by heredity will develop a foundation during those two years. Most of our beliefs about our Self form at this time and remain unchanged right up to our last breath. If we should find ourselves in a dysfunctional environment at this time of our lives, our survival odds diminish.

During those crucial first two years, our primary mission revolved around survival. In order to survive, we had to learn all we could about everything around us to know if it would help us or hurt us.

This remains true today. If you walk into a room of a hundred strangers, you have two questions, about every one of those strangers, that need answering. Each of those strangers also has the same two questions about you that need answers. When confronted with an unknown person, place, thing or situation, the very first thing any of us need to know, from a survival point of view, concerns whether or not that thing can hurt us. That first question always requires an immediate answer. Can it hurt me? The second survival based question just flips the coin over: can it help me?

Some adults and most young children also have a third question begging for an answer: what can I get away with? How far can I go? They need an answer in order to know the truth about the other person's boundaries. They usually want to know in order to discover if and how they can take advantage of that other person.

So there you stand, before the hundred strangers. How do you, and they, get the answers to such important questions? You can't very well engage each and every one of them in conversation to probe their innermost thoughts, feelings and intentions regarding you. You don't have the time or the opportunity. Neither do they, in order to get their questions answered about you. A dilemma, you say? Not really. Everyone got their answers. You did and they did. How? By observing. And when did we all learn that observation of a person's actions reveals the beliefs behind those actions? During those all important first two years of our life.

Remember, we had very little understanding of other people's formal, complex language to provide answers for us during those two long years; yet we desperately needed information. How did we go about getting what we needed? Of course, by observing people's behavior: by observing their actions in order to discover the beliefs behind those actions and whether those beliefs could hurt us or help us.

We learned to observe the behavior of others in order to discover truth. We did a lot of observing during those first two years. We have done a lot since then too, of course, but never as intensely as during that early period of our lives. We had an acute need to know what could hurt us or help us. We did not have sufficient knowledge of a mature, formal language which could convey any of that vital information to us or enable us to ask for it.

Observation and direct sensory experience made up our childhood survival tool box. If we touched a hot stove, our direct sensory experience told us a hot stove could hurt us. We also had to observe the people around us very closely in order to see if their behavior could hurt or help us.

We easily observed all the big and the obvious in other people. We also observed the subtle and the implied. It didn't matter what words our parents used, since we couldn't fully understand most of them anyway. We watched their faces and listened to the tone of their voices for subtle signs; and we watched their bodies for the more obvious signs. We watched all their actions like starving hawks circling their prey.

Since language, as we understood it then, conveyed only very limited meanings, we also tuned in directly to other people's feelings in order to obtain information. We needed to know anger in someone else because their anger could hurt us. We needed to know happiness in someone else because that could benefit us. Our

Pre-language

survival absolutely required us to have access to other people's emotional states, and so we opened ourselves up to it.

Nothing on this earth had the intensity of our emotional radar during those first two years. Nothing escaped us. If emotion existed anywhere within a parent, we picked it up. We easily tuned in on the obvious emotions, the ones they actually displayed to us.

We also tuned in on their repressed emotions. We felt them. Consider that. Our parents had repressed, denied and buried certain emotions and had, for all **their** intents and purposes, eliminated them. They could no longer feel them. Therefore, for them, the emotions didn't exist any longer. But we picked them up! We felt them! Wave after wave of their repressed rage, fury or sadness could flood over us and we had no way to stop it from affecting us. Our emotional radar had no 'off' switch then. We needed to know their emotional state in order to survive and so we made ourselves vulnerable to it. We came to experience a lot of things that our parents had chosen to drive out of their conscious awareness, right into ours. They could hide from their rage, their pain and their anguish, we couldn't. We had to remain in the flames, or the ice. At that age, we had no escape.

I will talk to you about the consequences of this later on.

An Ultimate Truth

44

Leveling the Field

Actions give evidence of beliefs. Observing the actions of other people reveals their beliefs. As children, we observed other people and now we do the same as adults. We observe them closely to discover beliefs that might hurt or help us. As in my example of the hundred strangers who also needed to know if you would harm them or support them, other people constantly watch us to answer their own survival based questions: could we hurt or help them?

I indicated earlier that most people have no idea what the list of their own beliefs looks like. In light of what you have just read, do you see the danger in that?

For example: suppose you want to buy a mid-size, mid-priced, conservative vehicle. You talk to a sales person, the sales person listens to you. A skilled sales person will spend 90% of their time listening and only 10% of their time talking. Your sales person listens and observes you, very closely. If he or she listens and observes you carefully, they will see your choices in action. Knowing that actions reflect beliefs, it won't take long for them to get a pretty good picture of some of your beliefs.

Now the sales person has in their mind a list of some of your beliefs. Since you, like most people, have no idea what your list of beliefs looks like, and the sales person does, who has the power? Clearly not you!

You will probably wind up driving away in something you really wanted but couldn't possibly afford. The observant sales person simply discovered that you believe you really, really deserve to drive something more in keeping with your fantasies, not your reality.

You never had a chance.

An Ultimate Truth

If we walk around with no knowledge of our own beliefs, then anyone who observes us and, in so doing, learns some of our beliefs, has power over us. They will have power over us because we gave it to them by choosing to live accidentally; by choosing not to have full Self awareness; by choosing not to have knowledge of our own belief system. We victimize ourselves this way. People don't have to work very hard to turn us into victims. We make it easy for them. We turn our Selves over to those who would take advantage of us.

If everyone looks at everyone else's actions to learn their beliefs, doesn't it seem like a good idea to know what your own list of beliefs looks like? Then you would at least play on an even field; other people would know your beliefs and you would know your beliefs. No one would have an unfair advantage.

If you learn all of your own beliefs, you will definitely have a major advantage over every other living person. No other person can identify more than some of your beliefs, no matter how much time they spend observing you. Different people will pick up different beliefs from you. But if you have all your beliefs in your conscious awareness, no one person can have what you have and therefore you maintain your advantage in every situation.

Choose **un**awareness of your own beliefs and you will have **no** advantage in **any** situation. You will have stacked the deck against your Self by making such a destructive choice.

If your primary core belief says that your Self doesn't warrant protection, development or celebration, then of course you will choose to live in a trance, unaware of what you believe.

When other people victimize you, a great opportunity will present itself for you to trophy polish; to feel good by feeling bad; to play 'poor me'; to play the martyr; to embrace misery in order to obtain pity.

Any fantasy based belief will fail to help you survive in reality. A belief that says you don't need to have any awareness of your own belief system springs directly from a destructive fantasy.

45

Emotions, First or Second

In summary, beliefs carry the responsibility for creating 100% of our choices and, therefore, our voluntary actions. As we evaluate the reality of our options, we compare what our senses tell us with the beliefs about reality we already have in our head. In every sense, our beliefs create our actions. Conversely, our actions give anyone who cares to observe us evidence of our beliefs. If they observe us intently enough, our beliefs will become known to them. If they have knowledge of our beliefs and we do not, we lose our personal power with regard to that individual. They know us better than we know ourselves, therefore they can victimize us if they choose to. Consequently, it appears reasonable to know our own beliefs so that we can at least have parity with our observers.

I have also said that those same beliefs have a cause and effect relationship with virtually all of our emotional responses. Our beliefs activate our emotions. We still carry a few primeval emotional triggers within us from birth that function independently of our beliefs but they affect us only rarely. The remaining 99.9% of our emotions respond directly to our beliefs.

If we want to change our emotional state, we must change the underlying belief. Trying to change emotional states by thinking about our emotions won't work. We must think about the beliefs that activate them.

I often ask people if they classify emotions as primary or secondary. Primary means that they come first, that emotions can exist of their own volition. They can suddenly appear for no reason whatsoever. Nothing causes them, they have a life of their own.

Secondary means that something external activated them. We experience our emotions as the effect of a cause; they occur as a consequence of something else.

An Ultimate Truth

Since beliefs activate emotions, emotions result from a cause and qualify as secondary. I can offer you a simple, reasonable proof for this.

Recall my example of the spider walking in on three people. Each of them had different beliefs about spiders. You saw them as basically non-threatening. I saw them as dangerous. The third person saw them as friends. Different beliefs activated different emotional responses. Your emotions expressed ease and comfort. Mine expressed fear. The third person's expressed joy. Same spider, three totally different emotions resulting from three different beliefs.

Specific beliefs generate specific emotional responses. Think back to the last time you felt angry about something, anything at all. Why did you experience anger? What belief activated your emotion?

For example: somebody steals your car or robs your house or intentionally runs over your cat. Try to identify the deepest underlying belief that those experiences touch. The belief probably sounds like, "They shouldn't have done it. I believe that all people should treat me, and my property, with respect. Especially, they should treat my cat with respect."

Our beliefs fall into one of two categories: realistic or unrealistic. Realistic beliefs have their entire root system deeply buried in the soil of reality. Unrealistic beliefs have their roots in the clouds.

In my example, did the hypothetical belief I cited sound realistic or unrealistic? Remember, fantasies and wishes do not automatically transform into realities simply because they express **my** fantasies and wishes. My fantasy may very well express a wish that every person on the face of the earth will automatically treat me, and my property, with respect. In reality however, very few people will do that automatically. You may want people to treat you with respect but choosing to want something doesn't magically turn it into reality. If you feel hunger, you can't wish a meal onto your table anywhere but in your dreams.

Emotions, First or Second

I have already alluded to the fact that our beliefs can just as easily represent fantasy truths as they can represent truths based on reality. Remember that our beliefs express our truths. Fantasy based truth creates fantasy based beliefs. And, quoting myself again, "Intellectual dysfunction results from creating beliefs based on fantasy truths."

To carry it a little bit further, emotional dysfunction results from fantasy based, unrealistic beliefs activating our emotions.

Unrealistic beliefs can turn our emotional states into waking nightmares. They can totally dysfunction our emotions.

If I believe, unrealistically, that all people should automatically treat me with respect, I bring a curse of constant misery and anger down upon myself because, surprise, surprise, they won't automatically respect me. I know, I used to have such an unrealistic belief and I remember vividly the unhappiness my own belief caused me.

As anybody with an ounce of intellectual functionality and experience knows, we can only earn respect from others and it takes work to do it, lots of work. The notion that all the people in the world should see any individual as immediately and automatically deserving of respect practically defines megalomania; not a healthy belief.

I want to present an interesting question to you. How many steps precede an emotional experience? If feeling an emotion occurs last, in a chain of events, how many other events happen before we can feel something?

At least one, since we have to perceive that 'something' exists in a space where we had previously perceived either nothing or something else. Perception by our senses starts the ball rolling and delivers some information for us to consider.

So, we initially have perception and eventually the emotional experience: two steps. First we perceive something and then we have our emotional response to whatever registered with us.

An Ultimate Truth

Perception and response would seem to sum it all up very nicely. First we perceive something and then we have an instantaneous emotional reaction. Do you feel like adding any more steps between perception and emotional response?

I hope so. By what mechanism do we move from perception to emotion? Which of our faculties become engaged in the process? How do we get from 'A' to 'B'?

Perceiving that 'something' has entered our field of awareness merely indicates that our senses have registered some incoming data. We have to initiate another step in order to figure out what the data tells us.

Picture this. You sit alone in your living room reflecting on life in general. Your eyes vaguely focus on the floor directly in front of you. Your thoughts float in free fall. You engage your senses at a minimum level and maintain only a basic degree of connectedness to your immediate physical environment. Suddenly you become aware that 'something' has appeared on your floor, right in front of you. A moment before you only perceived 'floor,' now you perceive 'something' sitting on that floor. Step one: perception.

The 'something' you perceive has no particular shape. It just looks like a pile of green jelly that occasionally quivers. What step comes next? First you perceived the thing, now what?

You need to identify it. Step two requires you to attach some form of identification to that which you perceive. You have to know if 'it' will hurt you or help you.

Consider some of the possible labels you could attach to the green, wiggly stuff in order to identify it: an alien life form; something that crawled out of the back of your refrigerator; something your family pet coughed up; a particularly vivid, medication-induced, hallucination; etc.. You need to hang some kind of sign on it to define its identity. Let's say you decide to label it as an alien life form. You have completed step two.

Emotions, First or Second

First you perceived it, then you identified it. What next? Another step still separates you from the last step of an emotional response.

What beliefs do you hold concerning alien life forms? Instead of the word concept 'life form' we could easily substitute 'spider'. How do you feel about spiders? How do you feel about alien life forms? In both cases, **how** you feel depends upon the beliefs you hold regarding either one of them. Just like the spider example, you could believe that alien life forms will automatically harm you; you could believe that they pose no threat whatsoever or you could believe that they need love and affection. You will believe something about alien life forms. Whatever you believe will complete step three. Your evaluation of the alien involves comparing your sensory perception and identification with the beliefs you already have in your head about aliens. You will believe that they have attributes of danger, neutrality, friendliness or something else. You will believe in some kind of truth about them. That belief you hold will apply to the green thing sitting on your living room floor. If you believe it harmless, neutral or friendly, you will react accordingly, with an emotion 100% appropriate to your belief. As you experience your appropriate emotional response, you will complete step four.

First we perceive, our senses register 'something.' Then we hang a sign on our perceptions in order to establish some type of identification, even if the sign reads 'unknown,' we have at least identified it as such. Then we will apply existing beliefs to that which we have identified. Depending on which of our beliefs apply, we will experience an emotional response totally appropriate to the activating belief. All of this happens very, very fast and gives us the impression that we jump from perception to feelings, but we don't.

An Ultimate Truth

46

Stress Sources

Up to this point, I have discussed with you how our beliefs account for all of our choices/actions and virtually all of our emotions. Beliefs also determine whether or not a given situation will affect us psychologically as positive stress or distress. Positive mental stress, or Eustress, gets us up in the morning. We experience positive stress when we go on vacation, get married, engage in sexual activity or receive a promotion. Too much stress of any kind can kill us, positive or negative. Plenty of heart attacks occur during vacations or sex. Whether we initially see a stressor as positive or as distress depends entirely upon our evaluation of it.

As you know by now, evaluation compares what our senses tell us with beliefs already held in our head. Certain of those beliefs will apply to our sensory data and activate emotions appropriate to those beliefs.

As we evaluate life situations, our beliefs determine our emotional responses to any particular reality. Distress, or cognitive dissonance, occurs when the reality **outside** our head doesn't agree with what already exists **inside** our head.

Back to our spider with the three observers. You, who felt indifference, experienced neither positive stress nor distress. I definitely felt distress as I shot out the door. The other person felt motivated enough by positive stress to leap forward and embrace the spider.

If my beliefs never conflict with reality, I will never experience any psychological distress. For this to happen, I would either have to have no beliefs or absurd beliefs. If for example, I had a nihilistic belief that sounded like, "Nothing, including myself, matters or has any significance," then I would never experience any conflict with any external reality; my absurd, fantasy based belief would protect me. On the other hand, if I had no beliefs

An Ultimate Truth

whatsoever, about anything, my resulting vegetative state would also protect me from distress.

The next time you experience distress, ask yourself which of your deeply held beliefs disagrees with the reality you perceive. For example, If your boss makes unrealistic demands upon you, and you find that distressful, look into your head and find out which beliefs disagree with that reality.

For example, you will experience distress if you believe that, "My boss shouldn't treat me that way." That expresses an unrealistic belief. The idea that someone will behave a certain way just because you think they should reveals a belief based on fantasy. That notion has no basis in reality.

"My boss must see that I can't do this job without more help," expresses a belief based on the fantasy that your boss reads minds and knows everything.

"My boss shouldn't expect miracles from me," demonstrates a fantasy belief that expects all people to act rationally towards you.

"My boss should realize that I can't get this done in the time remaining." Maybe your boss does realize it. Maybe your boss doesn't care how much inconvenience you suffer. Your fantasy belief says that everybody will feel bad if they realize they have inconvenienced you. Reality says that very few people will care if they learn they have inconvenienced you.

If you have reality based beliefs, distress will not plague you. **If your beliefs have the 'killer words' of should, ought, must, always or never in them, they have their origins in fantasy.** I'll give you a lot more information on identifying your beliefs in a later chapter. For now, try to monitor your beliefs and see how often those killer words show up.

A final thought about realistic vs. unrealistic beliefs and distress.

Stress Sources

'Hope' expresses a realistic belief or expectation. "I **hope** my boss gives me a raise; *but he/she might not.*" The situation has odds of 50/50.

We can see the reality of the situation accurately and we **hope** for the outcome we want, **knowing realistically that it could go either way**. This represents a very healthy point of view.

"I **know** my boss will give me a raise" expresses an unrealistic belief: an unrealistic expectation. I really have expressed a whim, a wish, **a fantasy**. I don't **know** anything of the sort.

Unrealistic beliefs and expectations express fantasy truths.

"I **know** he/she really loves me" often expresses a fantasy rather than a reality.

So does, "I **know** nothing will go wrong," or "I **know** I'll never get caught." "It doesn't bother me, who cares!" almost always expresses a fantasy.

With these unrealistic fantasies, and many others, we set our Selves up for disappointment, denial and unnecessary distress. I **hope** you agree.

An Ultimate Truth

47

Percentages of Reality

How well do you perform the task of accepting reality as real? I don't mean how well do you knuckle under and accept all the garbage life throws at you. I mean how well do you accept the truth, about what really exists, into the picture you have of your world. Especially, **how well do you accept reality that you hate, loath and despise**?

If I have a client who has an overeating disorder, I usually start them out with a test. I ask them to go home, stand in front of a full length mirror nude and then come back and tell me, generically, what they saw. Many of them report that they couldn't actually focus on every part of their body in the mirror out of embarrassment or disgust. They couldn't accept the reality of certain overweight parts of their body. They couldn't 'see' those parts until they reduced in size. I have to tell these people that no one can help them at this point.

They denied the existence of fat, at least on themselves. If fat does not exist in their real world, then nothing they will do in their reality can have any effect on fantasy fat.

We can't change something unless we can acknowledge its existence. We can't reach into a dream at will and rearrange the furniture. I can't recover until I admit I have something to recover from. Denial means that something doesn't exist in my real world. If it doesn't exist in my real world, how can I affect it? If my client's fat cells don't exist, to them, then they have no reason to attempt to change anything. They have to look at every extra ounce they carry and accept it as real, even though they may hate, loath, despise and abhor it. They don't have to like the reality they see, they just have to accept it as real. If they can accept it as real, they have a chance at weight loss. If not, it will never happen.

An Ultimate Truth

You and I have the same responsibility, to ourselves. We can choose to see reality as real, with all of its imperfections, we can choose to see none of it or we can choose to see only a part of it. The part we choose **not** to see will guarantee the continuation of our dysfunction. That unseen part of our reality, the part we choose to deny, will end up in some created fantasy where it will remain safe from any of our efforts to reach it and change it. Stuffing a piece of our reality into a fantasy makes it untouchable.

Can you accept **all** the reality you perceive as real, even though you might hate some of it?

The extent to which you deny even the smallest part of your reality will make that part of your dysfunction forever unavailable to you. It will remain safely protected by your fantasies and impossible to change. How can we change something that doesn't exist in reality? We can't.

How do you see your reality? Do you see it as all or nothing, black or white or do you see it as shades of gray, in degrees of variations?

Let me show you a model that I developed. Every time you find yourself in a 'situation,' think of this model. It will help you. What do I mean by a 'situation'? I define a situation as any block of sensory data that registers in your conscious mind as a discrete unit, separate from any other discrete units. Think of a situation as a chunk of reality, focused on one primary topic, that has continuity of sensory content.

When you get up in the morning, when you drive your car, when you give a speech, when you have an argument, when you watch a sunset, when you buy a meal, when you take a bath, when you hug a child; all these qualify as situations you could find yourself experiencing. Any segment of your reality that has intrinsic continuity, hangs together and focuses on a primary topic qualifies as a situation. For example, as you read these words, you find yourself experiencing a 'reading' situation. You will remain in this 'reading' situation until you choose to do something else. Then you will experience that other situation. For example, you

Percentages of Reality

might get up and enter a 'going to the bathroom' situation at any moment. Reality consists of a continuous stream of situations, one after the other, every day of our lives.

Now, for the thing that matters to us in our quest for functionality: how do we see each of these situations in which we find ourselves?

Visualize any particular situation as a 100% reality. Do you tend to see it as 100% positive? Do you tend to see it as 100% negative. Do you generally see it as a combination of positive **and** negative?

If you see reality dysfunctionally, each situation will appear to you as either 100% positive or 100% negative, with no gray areas in between. If you see the reality of every situation as some combination of both positives **and** negatives, you see it functionally and you see it from a healthy perspective.

How we choose to see reality separates function from dysfunction and separates survivors from victims. I can't overemphasize the crucial importance of this process. The model requires us to see every situation as it really exists, whether we like it or not.

For example, assume you experience a situation in which you find yourself looking at the termination of a long relationship. You don't hate your partner, but love no longer binds the two of you together. You will soon separate and end your connection as partners. You have very mixed emotions. You remember vividly the happiness and the pleasure you experienced over the years and, of course, you have equally clear memories of the pain, the suffering, the arguments and the recriminations.

Logically, the relationship could not possibly have sustained a 100% negative condition or it would have ended a long time ago. Conversely, It could not possibly have maintained a 100% positive status either, since you both have human characteristics and human emotions. Some rain must occasionally fall in a real world.

An Ultimate Truth

The same logic says that no situation can have a 100% positive or negative character. The worst situation you can imagine won't last forever, and the happy fact that it won't last forever adds a small positive element to the total picture. You could experience a 99% negative situation and it would automatically have a 1% positive component because of the good news that it can't last forever.

The exact same ratio applies to a positive situation as well. Since reality says that, sadly, a positive situation can't last forever either, we can only experience a 99% positive situation coupled to a 1% negative component.

So it appears that our maximum positive or negative experience, within any given situation, looks like a 99%/1% blend in either direction. To split hairs, you could certainly make it 99.99%/.01% just as long as we could attribute **some** part of the total situational experience to the fact that, whether positive or negative, it can't last forever.

A positive or negative situation of **maximum** intensity would register as a combination of 99% and 1%. **All of our situations blend into a mix of positive and negative experiences. Only the percentages change!**

A 50/50 situation would have equally positive and negative parts. The old joke about watching your mother or father in-law drive off a cliff in your brand new car personifies the mixed emotions of a 50/50 situational reality. 50/50 personal relationships can easily go on for a lifetime just so long as nothing significantly unbalances the ratio of positive and negative experience.

51% positive, 49% negative expresses a **slightly** positive situation. 95% positive, 5% negative expresses an **extremely** positive situation.

What kind of day did you have yesterday? Look at everything positive that you experienced and also look at everything negative that you experienced. **Do not, under any circumstances,**

Percentages of Reality

ignore or deny anything. In this example, the time period 'day' defines the 'situation' that you experienced. How did the scales tip yesterday? Perhaps you had a 60/40 day. Not bad, (positive/negative). If you had a really rotten, miserable day, you probably had a 10/90 day. Sorry to hear it.

How did your first date with a new person go last night? 90/10, congratulations. 10/90, sorry. What did you think of the last dinner you had at a new restaurant? 80/20, you'll probably eat there again and recommend the place to your friends. 15/85, you probably won't even walk your dog past the place in the future.

You really enjoyed the class you took, you got along well with all the other students, you made many new friends and the knowledgeable instructor gave you a lot of new information that helped you get a promotion at work. Of course you still had to pay a lot to attend, the seats seemed designed to cripple you, the temperature of the class room either froze you or fried you and you had to travel miles to get there. You call the percentages on this one.

Back to that dissolving, long term relationship. How will we look at that? The same way we look at every other situation. We have to clearly identify the positive and negative percentages. We must recall the terrific stuff **and** the terrible stuff. Since the example pictures a relationship ending, the ratios which apply to that relationship must range from 49/51 to 1/99. We absolutely must **not** deny any of the realities of the past relationship if we want to remain healthy and functional. No matter how horrific a relationship has become, at one time it had to contain some positive moments, if only in the very beginning.

I admonish my clients to look back at their relationships with clear and accurate hindsight. The negatives they see will explain the reasons why the relationship ended. The positives they see will explain why they feel so sad and miserable even while celebrating the end of a predominantly negative relationship. Positive moments remain as positive memories. Surrounding them with memories of negative moments doesn't negate the reality of

An Ultimate Truth

the positive moments. No matter how bad things got, **some** moments will always remain beautiful and memorable for us. And, we will miss those beautiful moments, we will grieve their loss and we will mourn their passing, just like we would grieve and mourn the loss of anything else we had reason to value.

This model requires us to see reality with all its beauty and all its ugliness. The mix of the two aspects expresses the truth of reality, whether we like it or not and whether we choose awareness of it or not. Dysfunction prevents us from accurately assessing the situations in which we find ourselves. Dysfunction causes us to look at our situations through a screen woven of fantasies, dreams and magic. We all enjoyed that experience as babies. As adults, continuing the charade will only result in Self destruction.

48

Consciousness, Above and Below

Speaking of how we view reality, I want to talk to you about how our brain works. It will help if you think of a brain as a building with three floors. The top floor represents our conscious mind. The middle floor represents our below-consciousness mind. The bottom floor represents our maintenance department.

The bottom floor has all the equipment that keeps us going without our having to think about it. This level keeps us breathing while we sleep, keeps our digestive system working after we've eaten and generally makes sure that everything our brain and body needs to do, in order to keep us alive, continues to go on without any help whatsoever from our conscious mind.

The top floor, where our consciousness resides, resembles a big, crowded, totally dark room with no windows. Visualize our consciousness as a flash light with a narrow, bright beam. When we activate our consciousness, we activate the flashlight in the dark room.

I portrayed the room as crowded. All the stuff our senses dump into the room every day accounts for the crowding. What we see, hear, smell, taste and touch piles mountains of information into the room.

When we activate our consciousness flashlight, we can only shine it on one spot at a time. As we slowly move the beam around in the otherwise total darkness, some of the stacks of sensory data gradually come into view. Then we see things more clearly as the flashlight hits the stack straight on, then gradually our awareness of that particular stack fades as the beam moves on to other heaps of data. **We can only experience that which our consciousness illuminates**. Everything else must wait its turn. Our little flashlight can not light up the entire dark room at once. It can only brighten one small spot at a time.

An Ultimate Truth

Interestingly, the contents of the room keep coming and going. New sensory information keeps coming in. Old information keeps decomposing and turning to dust in the corners of our room, never to reappear. The flashlight of our consciousness only picks out one small part of a constantly changing landscape at a time.

Occasionally, our light will hit a pile of data in the dark that interests us. Our interest motivates us to spend some time rummaging through the contents. We choose to stay focused right there for a while. We bring a great deal of the sensory data out into our light to see what it looks like. We temporarily bring some of the information into our conscious awareness in order to spend some time looking at it, enjoying it, learning from it or evaluating it. Eventually we will move our light away.

If the information we have momentarily retained in our consciousness has had any significance for us, It may slide out of our consciousness, through a trap door in the floor, and wind up as part of a growing mountain of data slowly accumulating in the darkness of the middle floor. That mountain makes up our below conscious mind.

Once data has dropped through the trap door, it no longer remains in our consciousness. The data still exists, but it now has a new home in that part of our mind which remains virtually inaccessible to our conscious mind. We can't shine our flashlight through the trap door and see into the middle floor. It always snaps shut after letting something through. Dreams symbolically access it and hypnosis may bring something to light in certain individuals, but, for all intents and purposes, once our stuff drops down into the middle floor of our building, we can say good by to our conscious awareness of it.

You may have noticed how carefully I stick to the term 'below conscious' mind. I obviously avoid using the terms unconscious and subconscious. Unconscious and subconscious have, in my opinion, too many different definitions which depend upon the person using them or the school of thought backing them. In choosing to use 'below conscious' exclusively, I hope to avoid

Consciousness, Above and Below

uncertainty or lack of clarity. It simply refers to that portion of our brain that our conscious mind cannot access directly. It stores our memories, our impressions and our old beliefs. It originates our dreams. It allows our intuitive abilities to sometimes run loose and make connections that we otherwise wouldn't make consciously. Unfortunately, we can't get in and wander around inside the 'below conscious' mind at will.

An Ultimate Truth

49

Beliefs, Above and Below

Do you remember the 'dry sponge' analogy that I shared with you earlier? Our conscious mind, at birth, resembles a very, very dry sponge onto which every bit of incoming sensory data falls. We soak up new information at a tremendous rate. We start to fill the empty room of our conscious mind with as many piles of data as we can. We create a veritable flood of incoming perceptions. Most of it doesn't make any sense to us at that age but it keeps coming nonetheless. Once in a while, something will show up in the flashlight of our consciousness that interests us and means something to us. We will choose to stay with it for a few moments before moving on and we will allow the data to temporarily occupy our consciousness. If it has enough significance for us, it might shoot through our trap door and land on our middle floor, thus beginning our mountainous accumulation of below conscious data.

Beliefs do that. They form briefly in our consciousness and then drop into the tank of our below consciousness. They come into existence and, if they have any real significance to us at that point in our lives, they wind up 'downstairs.'

As I also mentioned earlier, this happens whether our beliefs evolved from fantasy based truth or reality based truth. The trap door makes no distinction as to the nature or the origins of the beliefs it allows to fall through. No guard sits at the gate, protecting our Self interests. Any garbage can get through that trap door. Until we reach seven or eight years of age, we have no power whatsoever to say, "Now wait a minute, that belief could hurt me, it looks like a destructive, unrealistic, fantasy based and dangerous belief. I sure don't want that thing sitting down in my below conscious mind for the rest of my life, causing me grief, pain, confusion and suffering."

An Ultimate Truth

Would that we could say such a thing, but we can't.

I really want you to consider what this means. It means that any belief can get into our below conscious mind during our first few years of life. **Any belief.** We don't start putting a guard at the trap door until our developing capacity to reason allows us to say "no" or "that doesn't make any sense to me and I won't accept it." That means we can't put a protector at the door for seven or eight years. By the time we can put one there, we may have accumulated seven or eight years worth of destructive, fantasy based beliefs. They will remain unknown and unavailable to us for the rest of our lives unless we dig them up.

We will definitely become aware of their existence, however, as they cause us to make more and more dysfunctional choices.

Once an early belief drops into our below conscious mind, it will still cause us to act upon it, we simply won't know why we make the choices we do. Those beliefs will still drive and motivate our choices from their protected sanctuary.

We just won't know that they live there.

Consider the trap door. In those early years of our life, absolutely nothing will prevent a belief, developed in our conscious mind, from sliding through the trap door: down into the dark mass of stuff we've since forgotten. People often ask the question, "How can beliefs I don't even know I have make my life miserable today?" The key lies in part of the question, "I don't even know." Our conscious mind lost track of those old beliefs a long time ago, when they dropped through the trap door and took up residence in our below consciousness. Once there, they still determine our choices, actions and emotional responses.

Any time we make a choice or feel an emotion that we can't tie to a conscious belief, we have proof of the existence of a buried belief, alive and well below consciousness, still pulling our strings. Repressed emotions reach out like that and grab us from hiding; so do old beliefs.

50

Hidden Drivers

As babies and very young children, we reached conclusions, established reality based truths or fantasy based truths and formed beliefs expressing those perceived truths. Any of those beliefs that had significance for us at that time could have slipped through the trap door with no guard and become a part of our below conscious mind. Once there, they influence us exactly the same way conscious beliefs influence us.

For example, suppose you have a strong conscious belief that cockroaches have no value and deserve to die. You **know** that you have that belief. You have total awareness of it. You give the world evidence of your belief by your actions. You choose to squash a roach every time you see one. You go out of your way to jump up and down on roaches. Anyone observing you would have ample proof that you believe that roaches have no right to share the same earth with you.

All right, your aggressive anti-roach behavior puts your belief into action. You see your own belief with full and conscious awareness. How about an example of a belief that you do not know you have? How would you know you had a buried belief if you had no consciousness of it? Easy. You would see the results of your unknown belief in the choices you make and the emotions you feel for which you can not find an originating belief. When asked why you chose to do something, you would give the honest answer, "I don't know." When you experience an emotion for which you can not find an originating belief, you have proof that the belief lies below consciousness. It has to. You don't have the conscious knowledge of the belief behind your choice or your emotion, yet you made the choice or felt the emotion. Your experience proves the existence of the belief. Your lack of conscious knowledge as to its origin provides the location of the belief.

An Ultimate Truth

Do you look both ways before you cross a street? Probably. Why? What old belief do you have that causes you to choose to look both ways before crossing a street? You probably don't consciously know. Yet you act on an unknown belief. You know where that unknown belief lives now.

What suddenly brought tears to your eyes when you watched that late night movie? You certainly hadn't planned on crying. When your partner asked you why you cried, you honestly didn't know.

If an authority figure confronts you, why do you seize up and have trouble breathing and thinking straight? You have no idea what belief lies behind your physical, intellectual and emotional reaction. You have plenty of evidence of a belief at work but which belief? You don't know.

In groups of people you feel inadequate and suffer from anxiety. Where does that come from? You don't know. You do not have a conscious awareness of your underlying belief. Now at least you know the location of the belief.

In the following chapters, I will talk to you about finding those old, unknown beliefs in your below conscious mind. I will describe a process for identifying them and show you how to do it. I will show you how to create a different belief. I will then show you how to overwhelm a destructive, old, conviction with a constructive, new, rational belief.

51

Action Beliefs

How do we identify our old, hidden beliefs? How do we find them? Since we have no conscious awareness of them, what points in their direction?

Emotions and choices. Our choices point in the direction of our beliefs, known or unknown, and so do our emotions.

Let's start first with emotions. Our emotions point in their direction. Beliefs form from conclusions regarding truths. The process of belief formation represents an intellectual activity. The belief that slides into our below consciousness had its origin in our intellectual aspect. It came from our head.

You know that beliefs generate emotions. We have already discussed that. Conversely, our emotions provide evidence of our beliefs. A solid bond links beliefs with emotions and our intellectual aspect with our emotional aspect. If beliefs point towards emotions, then emotions point towards beliefs, specifically the beliefs that caused us to experience a particular emotional response.

If you want to start locating your hidden beliefs, start by keeping track of your emotions. Your emotions represent clues to the mystery your detective work will soon solve.

If you feel a significant emotion, identify the situation you found yourself in when you felt it. We've talked about situations. Your feeling will represent an emotional response to the belief you hold regarding the situation in which you find yourself. **Your beliefs apply to situations**.

We have an easy formula to follow. First, you feel a significant emotion. Second, identify the situation in which you found yourself when you felt the emotion. Third, ask yourself what you believe about that situation.

An Ultimate Truth

For example, you find yourself in a situation where you must speak in public. Studies have shown that speaking in public has a higher fear factor than death for most people. So you have identified your situation: someone has asked you to speak in public. You experienced the emotion of fear as a result of that situation. Now, what do you believe about that situation? What do you see as the truth regarding it?

Remember, our hidden beliefs can manifest either reality based truths or fantasy based truths. When you ask yourself what beliefs you hold regarding that situation, don't automatically go looking for a rational, reasonable, reality based belief. The odds favor a fantasy based belief. **Our fantasy beliefs most often wind up buried in our below consciousness because they find no support in reality.** If reality won't support them, they have to go where they will find support and acceptance. Anything goes in our below conscious mind, so fantasy beliefs find a home there.

What do you believe about the situation? Speaking in public and fear may seem welded together for you. What beliefs do you hold regarding the activity of public speaking? More specifically, what beliefs do you hold regarding **you** speaking publicly?

"I believe that if I get up and speak in front of a lot of strangers I will _____ ! Fill in the blank with as many possible completions as you can. You might believe that you will: faint; throw up on the podium; lose control of your bladder; lose your notes; trip and fall as you walk up to speak; say something embarrassing; forget your name; forget your speech; lose the ability to use a language; have your jaws suffer a sudden attack of disabling paralysis or have your tongue cleave to the roof of your mouth.

Your list will express your beliefs.

A comment before going further: you must do this work alone. No one can play therapist for you in this instance. If you choose not to do the work, you choose to remain ignorant of your beliefs. If you choose to remain ignorant of your beliefs, then

Action Beliefs

others will easily victimize you because they will learn about your beliefs by observing you and if they know your beliefs and you don't, they will have power over you. If they have power over you, they might cause you to suffer pain. If they cause you to suffer pain, who do you blame? You made the choice, you set the stage for your own suffering. Responsibility roosts on your shoulders, no one else's. I can't reach out of this page and force you to choose to work in your own Self interest. Nobody can. Only you can fight this battle for your survival, your recovery, the celebration of your life. You chose the beliefs you hold in the first place. If you believe that the job of finding and changing destructive beliefs somehow falls on shoulders other than your own, **that** destructive, fantasy based belief will destroy you.

If you choose to do the work, and decide not to trash this book at this point because the author has pointed out that your life rests in your hands alone, then you will observe that you came up with quite a few possible beliefs to explain your fear of public speaking. You have identified **action beliefs**. We act on them to get what we want. If you panic at the thought of speaking before a group, what do you want? You probably want to **not** have to do it. You probably want to get out of it. You probably want to avoid it at all costs. What do you believe you will have to do to satisfy your wants? Probably you believe that you must convince the person who asked you to speak that you can not or will not do it. You want to get off the hook. In order to convince that person, you have to trot out all the disastrous things you believe will happen if you get up to talk. You have to say to that person "I believe that if I get up and speak in front of a lot of strangers I will _____ !" And, then you will fill in the blank with as many of the beliefs from your list as you can in order to convince him or her of your unsuitability.

I said much earlier that under our action beliefs lie **core beliefs**. We have thousands of action beliefs. We only have a few core beliefs. You could probably count all your core beliefs on the fingers of two hands, and maybe a few toes. Each core belief breeds many, many action beliefs: sometimes dozens and sometimes hundreds.

An Ultimate Truth

Let's look at the hypothetical situation I asked you to see yourself fearing: public speaking. You fear that situation. That emotion of fear came from a core belief.

The way to reach and identify the underlying core belief requires you to look at **why** you believe you don't want to speak in public in the first place, why you believe you want to get out of it and why you believe you want to avoid it at all costs. Those action beliefs all manifest a simple, deeper, more profound core belief.

For example, if you had a core belief stating that, "I never have anything valuable to say," or "If I open my mouth, people will think I sound stupid," or "I don't deserve to have people listen to me," or "I feel ashamed when people look at me," you can clearly see why you wouldn't want to expose your vulnerability to strangers.

Core beliefs connect to action beliefs through the word concept, "**Therefore**." Because I believe 'x', **therefore** I believe 'y,' states it another way. Because of this, that.

Let's pick a core belief, one of the examples I gave you. Suppose the core belief stated that, "I feel ashamed when people look at me." Let's link that core belief up with some of the many action beliefs that could reasonably flow from it.

I feel ashamed when people look at me, **therefore, I believe that:**

- I should not speak in public.
- I must never let people get too close to me.
- I have to always try to seem invisible.
- I should wear big hats to cover my face.
- I can't encourage eye contact.
- I must wear clothing that covers me completely.
- I should sit rather than stand.
- I have to bury my shame.

Action Beliefs

- I must have something to hide.
- Other people see something terrible in me.
- Other people can see the awful truth about me.
- Other people will hate me if they see me.
- I must have done something horrible.
- I should avoid people.

I won't go on forever. I could. I could fill page after page with action beliefs that could reasonably flow from this one core belief. I hope you see the power of the core belief in this example. It can propagate innumerable offspring.

Depending upon our unique personality, genetic preprogramming, environment and experience, we will develop our own special list of action beliefs around our core beliefs. We will act uniquely. Nothing can determine in advance how a given individual will respond to a core belief and nothing can determine what that individual's list of action beliefs will look like. By the same line of reasoning, nothing can foretell what core beliefs an individual will develop either. We all have the potential to play unlimited variations on the theme of human behavior.

So, emotions can lead you to your beliefs. So can choices, as I said. Choices result from evaluating options. Evaluation, as a process, compares perceived reality with our internal reality in the form of our beliefs. Choices reflect beliefs. Actions, which result from choices, provide evidence of our beliefs. Look at your actions, your choices, your evaluations and your beliefs, in that order, to find your action beliefs. It requires just a little more work to dig one layer deeper to find the core beliefs.

Remember, the hidden core beliefs that influence us the most came from the earliest part of our life. The oldest ones express beliefs about us, our Self and our own value.

In my example, The core belief that, "I feel ashamed when people look at me," sounds like one of those old, deeply buried beliefs about Self that typically come out of a dysfunctional family

An Ultimate Truth

environment. It has all kinds of possible connections to sexual abuse and emotional abuse. I created hypothetical core beliefs for my examples but I took their essence from my direct experience with clients.

52

Core Beliefs

To bring past information to bear on the present moment, do you remember the content of the most significant core belief a person can have? Can you recall the core belief we discussed earlier that, "Affects more of your choices, emotions and actions than any other belief on your list?"

Right. Hopefully you recalled the core belief that, "Expresses what you see as truth regarding the 'most important thing you know'." I talked to you about the importance of this core belief.

If you believe that you, your life, your existence represents your highest value, you will survive dysfunction and live to celebrate every moment of your life.

If you believe that **anything** else represents 'the most important thing you know,' you will remain a victim of your dysfunction for the rest of your days.

Let me give you a graphic demonstration of the power inherent in this particular core belief.

For clarity, I restate the most powerful core belief on our list as, "I deeply and profoundly believe that I define the most important thing my senses can perceive as _____."

Now, you can fill in the blank in one of two ways. You can fill it in with what we have discussed before, "me, my life, my existence," or you can fill it in with anything else. Let me show you what happens in either case.

If the core belief says, "I believe that I define the most important thing I know as me, my life, my existence," the following action beliefs could reasonably flow from it:

An Ultimate Truth

Therefore, I believe:

- that I will protect that which I value so highly.
- that I will develop all my boundaries.
- that I will protect my health.
- that I will seek out people who add value to my life.
- that I will avoid destructive people.
- that I will not put poisons into my body or my mind.
- that I will rely on reason as my primary survival tool.
- that I will make sure I distinguish fantasy from reality.
- that I will value the existence of others since I value my own existence.
- that I will work to earn the respect of other people.
- that I will develop the skills and abilities I have.
- that I will celebrate the fact of my existence.

The list could continue, obviously, but you get the picture. Now, what would my action belief list look like if my core belief devalued my own life and diminished my own existence? What if my core belief read, "I believe that I define the most important thing I know as **anything but** me, my life, my existence?"

Therefore, I believe:

- that I have no particular motivation to protect my life.
- that I can easily put anything else before my Self.
- that developing my Self or my abilities has a low priority
- that anyone else's life has more value than mine.
- that I can poison my Self since it doesn't really matter.
- that I need not respect other lives either.
- that I shouldn't waste energy valuing my Self too highly
- that fantasy will help me to better understand reality.

Core Beliefs

- that other people have all the answers if I can just find them.
- that if I can find the right magic, I'll enjoy happiness.
- that boundaries don't matter: mine or anybody else's.
- that approval matters most when it comes from others.

Value your life and live. Devalue it and die. You pick.

To summarize the way beliefs work, we start out with opinions, or impressions that eventually settle down and form beliefs.

As we act on these beliefs over time, they become convictions. Repetition turns beliefs into convictions. A conviction defines a belief, strongly held.

We can base our beliefs on reality and we can base our beliefs on fantasy.

Some of our beliefs drop below our conscious threshold and disappear from view into our below conscious mind. From there, they will still affect us, even though we no longer have a conscious awareness of them.

Some of our older, deeper, more significant beliefs become core beliefs. We can't dig any deeper than a core belief.

Our core beliefs generate many, many action beliefs. We act on them. They form the bases of our evaluations.

They also activate our emotions. Our emotions will always reflect, with complete accuracy and consistency, the underlying action belief. To change our emotions, we must first change our beliefs.

To get at our old, buried, below consciousness beliefs we have two avenues to follow. We can follow our emotions back to the beliefs that activated them and we can follow our choices back to the beliefs that activated them.

An Ultimate Truth

Once we have identified our action beliefs, the real work of finding our core beliefs begins. When we find our core beliefs, changing them will automatically change all the action beliefs they generate. We don't have to change every action belief individually.

Since we all have thousands of action beliefs as part of our belief system, the fact that we don't have to go after them one at a time rightly sounds like good news. That would involve an awful lot of labor. The bad news, of course, emerges as we go about tracking down our few, but elusive core beliefs. That does involve a lot of work.

A word about changing beliefs. Each of us probably have a few healthy, constructive core beliefs that don't need changing. We will certainly want to retain them. Healthy beliefs generate healthy choices and healthy emotional responses. Our dysfunction can not survive healthy choices and healthy emotions.

But we can't decide which core beliefs to keep and which ones to change until we find them, hold them up to the light and see them clearly enough to make a rational, reality based, Self interested decision.

Actually, finding core beliefs requires a lot of grunt labor without demanding tremendous intellectual insight. The process won't make your brain sweat.

You will need a lot of paper to write down your action beliefs. Generate as many action beliefs as you possibly can. Write them down. Every time you feel an emotion, ask yourself what action belief activated it. Write down your answer. Every time you make a choice, write down what you believed true in your evaluations of your options. You will fill up many sheets of paper. I have described the grunt work.

Then, go over all your action beliefs on all your papers. Look for patterns. Look for beliefs that sound very similar to other beliefs. Look for beliefs that sound like another way of saying the same thing. Look for beliefs that point in a particular direction, and follow that direction to other, related beliefs. Keep alert for simi-

Core Beliefs

larities and equivalents. You will discover that great numbers of action beliefs, as a group, will begin to look more and more alike in concept. You want those concepts. Those concepts express the abstract equivalents of your core beliefs. Treat them like gold.

If you have living parents, listen to them. I once had a client who labored long and hard, searching for her core beliefs, and she found most of them. Then she confronted her father with unresolved issues. She did this at his office. His reply to her, the words and phrases he used, had a familiar ring to them. She took notes as he spoke. When she left, she sat in her car and compared her list of core beliefs, arrived at through much investment of time and energy, with her notes. By now you can guess what happened. They mirrored each other.

Since most of our old beliefs came from our parents, it doesn't require much imagination to see that the same parent will probably believe the same things today. Ask them about their truths, today. You might very well discover a genuine short cut to your own core beliefs.

If you do not have living parents, ask older relatives who knew your parents. Ask them if they can quote your parents' exact words and opinions about anything. See if they can remember specific statements or observations that each parent made frequently. Ask them what your parents thought about raising children. Inquire if your parents said anything about raising you, specifically.

Whether you wade through scores of action beliefs to find your core beliefs or whether you bring them to light all at once by listening carefully and closely to a living parent's words, persist until you have them. You will experience a strong, positive **or** negative, emotional reaction when you find one, so search with your heart as well as your head.

An Ultimate Truth

53

Common Dysfunctional Beliefs

As you search for your particular core beliefs, let me talk with you about core beliefs in general. I said earlier that each of us have thousands of personal action beliefs and that these action beliefs add up to a unique belief system that sets us apart from other people. Our particular belief system represents us and nobody else.

However, I also said that each of us have a very small number of core beliefs. Each core belief spins off great numbers of action beliefs. Let's say we each have around a dozen core beliefs, give or take. Dysfunctional people have certain core beliefs in common, more so than functional people. Functional people also have certain core beliefs in common, more so than dysfunctional people.

What characterizes a dysfunctional core belief? First, it will probably express an unrealistic expectation, with its roots in fantasy. Second, It will probably have the killer words of *should, ought, must, always or never* somewhere within the belief. Third, it will tend to express a global concept, such as 'every,' 'all,' 'no one,' 'none,' etc..

What beliefs do dysfunctional people often have in common? Actually, I did some informal research in order to answer that question. Over a number of years, I have periodically surveyed my audiences, my students and my clients to try and identify some common dysfunctional beliefs. I found a small group of beliefs that most people related to. Everyone I asked about the beliefs said that they all sounded familiar. Some suffered from almost all of them. I have never encountered anyone who didn't acknowledge either a past or present ownership of at least one of them. I'll present them to you and see what you think.

An Ultimate Truth

'Everyone should respect me.'

'Everyone should like me.'

'No one should hurt me.'

'No one should leave me or abandon me.'

'No one should ever hate me.'

'Everyone should acknowledge my existence.'

'I can't make a mistake.'

'Everyone thinks the same way I do.'

'No one can really trust me.'

'If people don't love me, I failed to deserve it.'

I purposely left one off the list because I must deal with it separately, in much greater depth. Our most powerful core belief defines 'the most important thing we know.' It influences more action beliefs than any other. Our second most powerful core belief defines the deadliest fantasy we could have. It has the second greatest influence on our action beliefs. That one I left off the list and we will get into it shortly.

How did you do with the list? Did you resonate with at least one of the beliefs? Did more than one grab you? Obviously, the wording of every belief could vary slightly according to individual interpretation. The message remains constant for each one of them though, regardless of the syntax. Do you now, or did you ever, own any of the messages on the list? The odds favor the probability that you did.

If any of the beliefs on the list I just gave you fit your list, feel free to add them and appreciate the short cut. My personal nemesis, many years ago, took the form of a belief that, "All people should learn as much as they can, from whatever source they can, all of the time." I believed this for myself, so naturally I assumed that every living, breathing human would have the same belief I did. In my defense, this occurred a very long time ago.

Common Dysfunctional Beliefs

My very unrealistic belief had killer words and global concepts galore. Bumping up against reality with a belief like that caused me to experience a lot of stress. Amazingly, people I ran into just didn't seem to go along with my belief. I generated a lot of 'cognitive dissonance' when the fantasy belief inside my head conflicted with the reality outside my head.

An Ultimate Truth

54

The Killer Belief

Now I want to talk to you about the second most powerful core belief we have; the one that has the second greatest influence on our action beliefs; the one that defines the deadliest fantasy we could have.

If a little child came running up to you and asked you to define 'perfection,' what would you say? What definition would you offer the kid? "I believe perfection _____ !" Of all the beliefs I have ever seen, this one causes the most frustration, anxiety and depression. Our primary core belief, 'the most important thing I know' determines the issue of life or death for us. If we choose to live, this second core belief can have the greatest negative affect on our overall, ongoing emotional condition.

That kid still wants an answer. I'll make it easy for you. In the first place, do you believe that the concept of perfection can exist in the real world? If you answered yes, big trouble looms on your horizon. If you said no, I want to explain the reason for your correct answer.

Where did the word-concept 'perfection' come from? How, when and why did it become a part of our language and, therefore, our thinking? Did our current civilization always have this concept?

In our Western culture, we can trace the idea back about 2500 years to the Greeks, to Plato in particular. The structure of his formal philosophy placed humans forever outside an ethereal world of perfect Forms and Ideas. The world of reality, where the people lived, could only receive inspiration and illumination from the world of perfect Forms and perfect Ideas. Plato never suggested that a living human could ever enter his world of unattainable perfection. That world had the job of showing people unachievable ideals. It let them see magnificent images that could motivate them

An Ultimate Truth

in their earthly striving and serve as models for emulation. He created a beautiful fantasy. He also made it very clear that people could never experience it. If they did, it would kill the perfection and make it mundane, secular and temporal. They would make it real. So the ideal world had to always remain an out of reach fantasy in order to fit the definition of 'perfection.'

Over the centuries since then, mystics, and those who profit from selling fantasies, moved a few people at a time into Plato's unattainable paradise.

Perfection in reality, in total contradiction of Plato, slowly crept into various Western cultures. Usually it rode in on the coattails of various religions.

Perfection served nicely to create 'them' and 'us' groups, the perfect and the imperfect, which made the mystics happy. Only the minority, comprising the 'select few', could enjoy the luxury of either achieving or benefiting from perfection. The 'imperfect' would, of course, represent the majority. The road to achieving 'perfection' naturally had some kind of cost and thereby empowered and enriched the mystics who 'had to' act as interpreters along the way, dispensing directions to perfection for a consideration.

The games of power and control the interpreters played, for so many years, served to force Plato's beautiful fantasy into people's reality and, in so doing, turned it into a destructive weapon.

Once an individual embraces the fantasy and accepts the notion that perfection can exist in reality, they fall victim to the people who define perfection and make the rules for its attainment.

If an interpreter decides to define perfection as something the victim can never attain, the victim enters a state of perpetual failure: failure to measure up, failure to meet standards, failure to deserve redemption, failure to feel 'good enough' to live, failure to deserve love and acceptance.

The Killer Belief

The victim can experience so much failure, in fact, that it drives them into a state of constant shame: enough shame to totally dysfunction them physically, intellectually, emotionally and spiritually.

A dysfunctional person makes an ideal victim. They tend to stay victims for the rest of their lives and continually enable those with the power and control to remain unaccountable for, and untouched by, their victim's suffering.

A parent can very easily become an 'interpreter' of perfection for a child. I have had client, after client, after client identify a parent, or parents, as someone who used perfection as a weapon. The parents set up impossible standards that guaranteed perpetual failure for the child. As a perpetual failure, the child suffered a constant sense of shame for their 'inadequacies.' In constant shame, they became ideal victims: totally dysfunctional yet protective of their victimizers. They saw their failure as proof of their unworthiness to live. Some chose not to.

Those who chose to live did so at great cost to their ability to protect, develop and celebrate their Selves. They became the walking, sometimes crawling, wounded. **Never 'good enough', they fell further victim to any distraction that promised relief from the pain of their unrelenting shame.**

Some of the most dysfunctional, shame based, addicted and Self destructive people I have ever met had perfectionistic parents who built walls too high for their children to climb. The parents then sat smugly behind those walls with their love, approval, vulnerability and acceptance forever unavailable to their kids. Most of the children nearly bruised themselves to death, emotionally, trying to get through a wall they couldn't climb. They all failed to penetrate their parent's walls and reached adulthood with the open wounds from their struggle unhealed. That much pain and shame needs a lot of distraction to cover it up.

I have seen plenty of evidence that many parents panicked as their children appeared to reach the top of the wall, **and they raised the wall!** They made it higher. No matter how high the kid

An Ultimate Truth

got, the parent added some more bricks to the top. **Perfection has that characteristic. The victimizer can always change the rules and automatically cause the victim to fail to meet new standards.**

Of course, a parent's own dysfunction motivated them to build the wall in the first place. Then, the parent's dysfunction passes on to the next generation as those children try, and fail, to achieve the impossible. Perfection becomes the weapon of choice for those wishing to keep kids away from the truth of their parent's dysfunction.

Withholding love, attention and acceptance always makes a child try harder to please the parent. When the child fails to please the parent, they believe that their own failings and inadequacies have caused the parent to reject them. Perceived rejection from one's own parents profoundly deepens their shame and makes the dysfunction even more dangerous and destructive. "If my parents don't value me, why should I?" And, for the most part, they won't choose to value themselves.

What alternatives do we have to perfection? If perfection can't exist in reality, what can exist in reality? **Degrees of achievement, excellence, accomplishment, satisfaction and pleasure can all exist in reality.**

In my favorite example, I say that if I really try, I can stand with my feet flat on the floor and jump about a foot in the air. I suppose that if I practiced jumping for years, I might add a couple of inches to my leap. So my top performance could possibly reach 14 inches off the ground. That height would express my upward limit, my maximum performance. It would represent, for me, a 100% achievement.

Now, if some professional athletes should wander by and see me jumping, they could laugh at me and make my effort look silly by comparison. They could probably leap four or more feet straight up into the air without even grunting. If they practiced for years, they could probably reach six feet above the ground. For them, six feet would express their upward limit, their maximum

The Killer Belief

performance, their 100% achievement. Four feet would represent some lesser degree of achievement.

Degrees, or percentages, of achievement express very personal parameters. The athlete's 100% performance dwarfs my 100% performance. Should I compare what I can do with what the athlete can do? Of course not. Degrees of achievement require a starting point **within the individual**. We can only realistically compete with our Selves.

Other people with greater or different abilities can inspire us to work harder to reach our own limits but they can't give us what we don't possess. The athlete jumping six feet into the air might inspire me to train harder but no amount of inspiration will magically give me the ability to exceed my personal capacities. Marveling at birds won't enable me to fly unassisted, no matter how hard I flap my arms. I have my limits in a real world.

If your parents used the weapon of perfectionism on you, It has probably contaminated you. You probably believe that perfection can exist in reality.

Do you have trouble achieving satisfaction, with anything? Does what you do never seem 'good enough?' If you can't achieve some impossible level of perfection do you give up completely since you must have 'all' or 'nothing?' If you think it remotely possible that you might reach some future state of achievement, do you start sabotaging yourself in advance to make sure that you don't measure up? Do you choose workaholism as your drug of distraction? Do you focus primarily on flaws and imperfections rather than on the total situation? Do you need to control people, at all times? Do you feel uncomfortable when things seem beyond your complete control? Do you need to have **everybody** think highly of you? Does rejection send you into deep depression or into an out of control rage?

I mention these as only a few of the signs that perfectionistic thinking has you in its unforgiving grip. If you believe, now, that perfection can exist in reality, all of the above, and more, might accurately apply to you.

An Ultimate Truth

I said earlier that this second most important core belief, "Can have the greatest negative affect on our overall, ongoing emotional condition." If you think that you can reach **any** state of perfection, under **any** circumstances, that destructive core belief will spin off hundreds of action beliefs that will activate countless destructive choices and emotions for you to experience.

If you choose to continue to hold on to such a belief, you choose to suffer. Remember, you did not come into the world with any beliefs. You acquired them. You can acquire new, healthier, more functional beliefs if you choose to. I will show you how to do it. In a coming chapter I will show you how to overwhelm an old belief with one that has more significance for you **now**.

But before then, I urge you to look very, very carefully at your present belief about perfection. If you believe perfection has a place in your reality, you dramatically diminish your chances for survival, celebration and independence.

You will remain a victim of every perfectionistic system that snares you in its web. You will never win, the interpreters of perfection won't let you. They will always raise the height of their walls at exactly the same moment you reach the top.

By clinging to such a destructive belief, you doom yourself to a lifetime of frustration and guaranteed, perpetual failure. You will certainly choose one option, one belief, from the many available to you. I personally hope you choose the one that best enables you to protect, develop and celebrate the most important thing you know.

55

Origins of Your Love

The most important thing we know: our most influential core belief. Our view of perfection, in or out of reality: our second most powerful core belief. We all have one more core belief in common and after that one, we all go our separate ways, to develop our own, unique belief systems. In total, these top three core beliefs represent, in my opinion, about 70% of our belief system in terms of power and influence. The remaining 30% of our system will certainly contain more than three core beliefs but, as a whole, they will not affect us as dramatically, as profoundly or as extensively as the first three.

My therapeutic approach directs me to discuss the first three common core beliefs with you in significant detail and also to lead you through a process by which you can track down the remainder of your core beliefs by yourself. We have almost completed this part. Then, I plan to show you how to change those beliefs if you determine that they no longer serve your Self interest or enhance your ability to fully function in all your four aspects. We only have our third, common core belief left to discuss. Any idea what it involves?

Love. Or, as I discussed with you earlier, our 'highest value.' Our belief about the nature of our ability to value reality has a tremendous impact on our formation of action beliefs and emotions, only slightly less powerful than the first two core beliefs we have already dealt with. What you believe about your definition of love profoundly affects relationships, not only with others but with your Self. It affects how, or if, you can love you. Then it affects how, or if, you can love others.

Your core belief about 'the most important thing you know,' determines whether, or how, you will live or die. Your core belief about the concept of 'perfection' defines your view of reality. Your core belief about love determines the nature of your relationships. Your top three core beliefs address the issues of: life/death; reality/fantasy; celebration/isolation. I think that qualifies as a potent group of beliefs.

How, when and where did we acquire our belief about the nature of love? Like all our other core beliefs, we first saw it take form in our earliest childhood years. I have seen the reality, that the model I will share with you represents, affect client after client, year after year. It affected me. It affected my wife, Deborah. It has affected every person I have ever worked with, either privately or in group settings. I feel pretty confident that it affects you.

One of my questions to every new client sounds like this: "Please describe how each of your parents related to you and what you remember them saying to you most often." I ask them to either speak or write their answer. I ask them to limit their response to a short paragraph or better yet, just a few lines. I ask for a separate statement about each parent. You might want to try this. You might want to stop at this point and jot down your answers to the question. I recommend it.

The way our parents treated us determined our definition of love.

For example, if you characterized your mother's behavior towards you as guilting, demanding, controlling and unforgiving and you characterized your father's behavior towards you as aloof, unavailable, emotionally detached or violent, you have everything in place for the formation of your own belief about the nature of love. Every child perceives those behaviors as 'loving' because they came from a parent.

Please don't say what so many people say, I beg you. Don't say that a child automatically has an intuitive definition of love that springs magically into existence at birth and enables the child to 'know' when people really love them, in spite of all the evidence to the contrary.

Origins of Your Love

The fantasy that says, "Daddy really loves me even though he beats me bloody, rapes me and humiliates me" or, "Mommy really loves me even though she knows my father abuses me and she does nothing about it," has no basis in reality.

No child has yet come into the world with a book in hand that tells them how to evaluate a parent's behavior and how to interpret it. Also, they certainly didn't enter the world with an all-inclusive omniscience enabling them to somehow see beneath a person's behavior and find some redeeming virtue that could excuse, ameliorate or in any way compensate for abuse.

What we receive from a parent will absolutely, positively register as an expression of love. Remember, our little lives depended upon these great big people. We couldn't allow our Selves to believe, at that age, that those who had our lives in their hands could do anything to us that would not demonstrate an expression of their high regard for us. We believed then, and, unfortunately, sometimes now, that anyone who has our existence in their hands **must** highly value us. As an unrealistic, destructive, fantasy based belief, that one ranks way up, or down, there with the worst of the worst. Fantasy beliefs and fantasy truths abound in children. If they persist into adulthood, they result in death and destruction.

But the child **does** believe that anyone who has their life in their hands highly values them: loves them. So the parent's behavior translates into loving acts. The child has no reason to evaluate the parent's behavior in any other way at that time. As they get older and see alternatives, they will, but not yet.

Back to my hypothetical example: from your mother you got guilting, demanding, controlling and unforgiving perfectionism. From your father you got aloofness, unavailability, emotional detachment or violence, Those characteristics got lumped together and became your definition of love. You believed that love had those characteristics.

I guarantee you that, unless you have changed your belief about your definition of love since your early childhood, you still hold that belief today.

An Ultimate Truth

Two things will happen to you, as a child. You will apply the definition of love you got, from the same gender parent, to yourself and you will also apply the combination of what you got from both parents to your relationships with other people.

As a female child, your mother modeled and exemplified your definition of love from a woman, which you then applied to your Self every time you looked in a mirror.

As a male child, your father modeled and exemplified your definition of love from a man, which you applied to your Self every time you looked in a mirror.

Your same sex parent showed you, by example, how to love your Self and what to believe about how to do it.

I also guarantee you that, unless you have changed that belief since childhood, you still love your Self in exactly the same way today.

Don't forget, as children we had no way to compare what our parents modeled for us with anything else we could refer to as 'normal' behavior. Whatever we received from our parents, we had to perceive as normal. We had no magic voice whispering in our young ears to tell us that what we experienced from them really deserved a definition of abnormal, abusive or perverted. We had to accept what we got as normal. We truly had no basis of comparison, in reality, to anything else. We only acquired alternatives as we grew older. As young children, whatever we experienced defined normalcy.

As a male, if your father detached himself from his children emotionally, you will believe it a loving act to detach your emotions from your Self. You will chose to experience emotional dissociation.

As a female, if your mother used guilt as a weapon of control, you will believe it a loving act to force feelings of guilt upon your Self. You will choose to experience guilt.

Origins of Your Love

Regardless of your gender, you will combine input from both your parents and create a composite belief about the nature of love as it applies to other people.

For example, if your father abandoned you and your mother controlled you with unearned guilt, that combination becomes your definition of love. When you eventually leave home, physically, you will look for someone to love. The definition of the love you want to find in another person will reflect the definition you carried with you when you left home. You will find a person who will abandon you and guilt you and you will absolutely believe that you have fallen in love. I have oversimplified my example, of course, but nonetheless I have described a very real situation for many, many people.

Victims of childhood violence often grow up to have relationships with violent people. That fact won't surprise anyone who hasn't lived in total isolation for the last forty years. Since it comes from a parent, violence upon young children can register with them as a loving act, even though it causes the child physical and emotional pain. Since a young child cannot conceive of a parent hurting them on purpose, out of malice or anger, the kid will often choose to believe that they must deserve the pain as punishment for some unknown wrongdoing. **They will choose to see themselves as the cause and the source of the abuser's violence. As long as the violence continues, the child will feel guilty for causing the parent so much displeasure.** If they live long enough to reach seven or eight years of age, they may then begin to question those beliefs, maybe. By then it may have gone too far for a child to correct with their newly acquired powers of internal reasoning. They will need external help and assistance, in that case.

If a child grows up believing that violence expresses a loving act, it doesn't take much imagination to understand why they would eventually chase after violent relationships.

I fell over the truth of this model many years ago when I had trouble understanding why two people in a relationship

An Ultimate Truth

couldn't seem to agree on anything that involved the expression of love and affection.

I finally, in desperation, asked them to individually define what love meant to them and how they felt it should reveal itself. Obviously I asked each one separately and privately. What an eye opener!

When I compared notes, I learned two important realities. One, I learned what I have shared with you, that we all have a different definition of love. Two, I learned why they had gotten into their relationship in the first place. **They initially satisfied each other's beliefs about the form an expression of love should take.**

As a child, his mother had related to him passively and submissively. In the beginning, so did his female partner in the relationship.

Her father controlled the family through rage and intimidation. Guess what characteristics her male partner exhibited during their courtship. Right, he had to control everything, no exceptions. He did it quietly, without all the shouting, but he still held her in an iron grip.

So, in the beginning, they fulfilled each other's definitions of love and each of them honestly felt 'in love.' Only as time passed did they begin to suffer from the pain of unmet needs as their limited fantasy beliefs came up against a bigger and deeper reality for which they had no functional preparation.

I suggest that you try out this model for your Self. Jot down how each parent related to you, as far back as you can remember, and also what you can remember them saying to you most often.

I had a male client to whom I gave this exercise and he replied that his father had abandoned his family in my client's infancy. He had no direct memories of a father relating to him in any way nor any memory of words a father could have spoken to him. I had the opportunity to point out to him that **his memory of the fact that** his father had abandoned him defined love from a

Origins of Your Love

man, for him. Not surprisingly, he became my client because he suffered from an inability to value himself or take himself seriously. I wonder why.

Most people who do this exercise express amazement at the correlation between their parents' treatment of them and their own definitions of love. This belief as to the nature of love has a profound impact on all your relationships. I strongly recommend you give it a try.

An Ultimate Truth

56

Times to Question

I suggest to you that we can all take a good hard look at our core beliefs three times in our lives. Two of those times float and have no assigned chronological point in our life cycle. The third time occurs at a more or less fixed point of time for everybody.

When do you think we first look long and hard at our beliefs? At what point in our lives do we first stop and reconsider our underlying, motivating beliefs? Would you guess that we will more likely question our beliefs in adolescence, upon entering college, upon entering military service, upon starting a new job, upon marriage, upon the birth of our first child?

Actually, any moment in time could motivate us to stop and evaluate our beliefs, as long as we perceive that moment as a crisis. Adolescence might result in crisis or it might not. It depends on the individual. The same applies to entering college, marriage etc.. For some, it may represent a crisis, for others it may not. A perceived crisis can occur at any time in a person's life. At that time, core beliefs come under very rigorous scrutiny.

All of us know someone, or know of someone, who suddenly and unexpectedly lost someone they loved. After the anger, the grief and the mourning, the survivor sometimes throws away many old beliefs and starts over. I had a Client who lost a brother in a hunting accident. She waved good-bye to him in the morning, wished him good luck, and never saw him again. After the shock wore off, she quit the job she hated, divorced her abusive partner, moved to a new State and asked me for help in adjusting to her new surroundings. I asked her why she made so many major changes in so short a time and she replied that, for her, the crisis of losing her brother so suddenly caused her to choose to look at every remaining minute of her existence and ask herself how she intended to spend it. On that basis, she saw no reason to continue

An Ultimate Truth

working at a job she hated, with a partner who abused her, in a State that depressed her.

A crisis always makes us look at time through a magnifying glass. We take time for granted until someone or something we value runs out of it. Then we suddenly take time very seriously. We count every second when a life teeters on the edge. We reevaluate our priorities at such a moment. We see, with new clarity, the precious nature of a moment of life.

Evaluation, as we have discussed, involves the application of our beliefs to reality. Reevaluating means that we evaluate the beliefs we already hold and see if they still serve our constructive Self interests. If not, we often make sudden and drastic changes in our action beliefs, on the spot.

Most of our core beliefs have formed by the time we enter school. We add a few action beliefs along the way as we grow older, but our core beliefs remain pretty well entrenched and untouched by our experience. We have all had things happen to us that caused us to change action beliefs in an instant. When we left home and ran into our first conflicts with new realities, we rejected a belief and replaced it with a new one in a flash. We all did some of this the first time we entered into a serious relationship with a partner. I guarantee that your beliefs about meals, sleeping times and arrangements, room temperature, visits by relatives, holiday rituals, sexual preferences and who-does-what around the residence raised at least some conflicts with your partner's beliefs. Military service has a way of confronting old beliefs and replacing them with new ones rather quickly; so does a serious illness.

Look back in your life. Try to recollect some of the old beliefs that you have changed when forced to. For example, the time you changed your adolescent belief that nothing could harm your bulletproof and immortal physical body; the time you changed your belief that you could get away with anything; the time you changed your belief that you possessed a job, a partner or a child for life; the time you changed your belief that drugs of choice would make everything better and take away the pain.

Times to Question

A crisis can cause us to look hard at our beliefs and, in many instances, change them at will. A perceived crisis, regardless of its intensity, can hit us any time, anywhere. Crisis points float through our lives and strike us without warning. By definition, we can't prepare for crises in advance. If we could prepare, it wouldn't become a crisis.

When do you think just about everybody reevaluates their beliefs? We all do it at more or less the same time of our life. Sure, retirement. When we chose to stop earning a living. Prior to retirement, we use most of our energy to work and raise a family.

As humans, we do not have unlimited energy. We must sleep every day. We get fatigued. We can't keep up a peak performance level forever. We have to stop to rest now and then.

Before our retirement, we allocated most of our energy to work and family. If you happen to enjoy the luxury of unlimited inherited income, with no need to work, you will probably expend all your energy on play. Even then retirement, chronologically, will present the same challenge to you.

Retirement tells us that we don't have the amount of energy we used to have; that we don't have to spend it all in work, family or play any more; that we approach the end of our life cycle; that we had some questions from our childhood that never got answered; that not having to work, raise a family or squander the family fortune any longer leaves us with more free time and relatively more energy available to fill that time.

A comment on the questions of our childhood. Most people had all kinds of questions to ask as children. You did. We all had the who, what, where, why, when and how questions on the tips of our tongues. We drove our parents nuts, for a while, with our questions. Eventually we all stopped asking. You stopped, I stopped. Why?

Two reasons. Either we got, "I don't know" so much that we gave it up or we got answers but we couldn't understand them. In either case, we eventually quit asking.

An Ultimate Truth

Professional philosophers make a living by attempting to answer the questions of children. They continue asking the questions, as adults, that most of the other kids stopped asking as children.

As we get farther from the beginning and closer to the end, the period of our life called retirement affords us an opportunity to go back and dredge up those unanswered questions from our childhood and possibly, finally, come up with some satisfactory answers. We can look closely at past and present beliefs to see if we can achieve some new level of understanding.

All right, that makes two times we look at our beliefs: after a perceived crisis and during retirement. What about the third time, the other floater?

The third time can occur any time you want. You can choose, voluntarily, to look at your beliefs **now** rather than wait for a crisis or retirement. The therapeutic process, that I describe throughout the pages of this discussion with you, can enable you to do it on purpose now, when you can benefit most from it. You can, of course, choose to wait for a crisis or retirement. I would encourage you to wait only if you can guarantee that you will survive the crises to come and that you will make it to retirement. If you can guarantee those things, then by all means choose not to do anything now.

This raises an interesting point, at least to me, and, I'll bet, to you as well. When I discuss the therapeutic work with people who have not yet gotten into it, they turn a little pale as I describe the amount of labor involved.

I explain to them that the work follows a simple, clear and understandable path, it simply does not travel over easy terrain. We encounter slippery slopes and steep, hard climbs. We dive into swamps and fight for high, dry ground together. Simple yes, easy no.

I frequently get a response that makes it clear the speaker sees their reality as a choice between doing the sometimes painful

Times to Question

work of the therapeutic process and not doing any work at all in order to avoid the pain. They see it as a pain vs. no-pain choice.

I then have to point out the following, to them, and to you. Presumably you presently experience some level of discomfort due to dysfunction or you would not have chosen to invest your time reading this far in the first place.

You have a certain amount of pain at this moment. This present pain you experience will not go away by itself. You can not grow out of it. No magical event will take it away from you. The pain will stay. As you grow older, the pain will increase, not decrease. I challenge you to assign pain points to what you experience now. For example, if your present pain causes you an estimated 30% of all the emotional pain you could possibly imagine experiencing, then use that number. Then add up the years you expect to live. Assign 30% pain to every remaining year and add an additional 10% to each of your last twenty years. Assign one point for each percentage of pain. This year, your pain counts for thirty points. It will get worse, so your last twenty years will result in forty points a year. Add up your total 'pain points' for the rest of your life.

If, for example, you have lived for thirty years already, you have a reasonable expectation of fifty more years of life ahead of you, barring accident or illness. The last twenty years of your life will count forty pain points a year, equaling eight hundred pain points. You can expect to experience your present pain level, of thirty pain points, for thirty more years. That equals nine hundred points. Add nine hundred to eight hundred for a total of one thousand, seven hundred pain points. **You will experience one thousand, seven hundred pain points if you do nothing**.

Let's look at the alternative. Doing what I call the 'work,' as described in these pages, involves some up-front emotional pain, possibly up to as much as you have ever experienced. If you characterize your present pain level at 30% again, for example, you might climb up to a few 99% pain moments. You will have many pain moments between 30% and 99%. Let's say you did the 'work'

An Ultimate Truth

for one year. It will help if you break the first year into months and come up with pain point totals for each month. Total your pain points for those months of that year, one point per percentage of pain. Add them all up. The second year, you will experience about half of the total number of pain points you experienced during the first year. Add that number to your total points from the first year. From the third year onward, you will drop to about a 5% pain level annually, meaning that you will carry about five pain points per year for the rest of your life. Add that to the previous totals from years one and two. Compare your total pain points from doing the 'work' to the total pain points you came up with from doing nothing.

Obviously this does not qualify as a scientific methodology and I do not present it as such. However, I do present this example, with these numbers and with these percentages, as an excellent rule of thumb, based on my experience with real clients, in real recovery situations, over many years. This 'pain point' model can help you to rationally determine your options. Most of all, it can show you, quantifiably, that the "pain vs. no-pain" concept has no basis in reality at all. **You just have to decide which pain you want.**

Choose to do nothing and retain your present emotional pain. Watch it increase as you get older. Choose to do the 'work' and experience some up front increases in your emotional pain, absolutely. We can't confront the stuff from our past without hurting. Watch the pain decrease as you do the work and watch it level out at a very low point for the rest of your life. Some pain must always remain in our awareness to motivate our vigilance. We can't forget all our pain or we won't have any reason to remain alert in the future. I will discuss vigilance with you later on.

57

How to Change Your Beliefs

Once you have identified a core belief, what comes next? You must then bring that belief up from the depths and look at it in the very bright light of day. Turn it around, look at it from every angle.

Once you have thoroughly examined it, you have two options. You can decide that the belief constructively supports your Self interest and keep it or you can decide that you want to get rid of it because it doesn't seem reasonable to continue to hold on to a destructive belief. If you choose to get rid of it, what then?

First, **you will never get rid of it**. Once those beliefs get into our personal program, they stay. No amount of work can kill an old belief. That sounds depressing, what can we do about it?

We can overwhelm the old belief with a new belief. How do we do that? **We act on the new belief, over and over and over and over.**

No magic will install a new belief in the place of an old one. No miracle will suddenly make a new belief yours. You will have to work at it: no short cuts.

Let me spell out the process. First, as we have discussed, you must identify the old, core beliefs that you have.

Second, bring one at a time out into the light for a good look.

Third, decide whether you want to keep that old belief or not. If you do, leave it alone. If you don't, then move on to the next stage.

Fourth, assuming that you don't want the old belief destroying your life anymore, you must create a new belief.

# An Ultimate Truth

Fifth, you must act on the new belief. Repeat as needed for each belief you no longer want. Return to stage four as often as you must.

Simple-but-not-easy really defines this fourth stage. To begin with, you must precisely define the old belief, in exact words. You have to have the old belief written down clearly in front of you before you can even think about creating a new belief to replace it. I cannot overemphasize the importance of doing this. If you just let the old belief rattle around in your head as some unformed concept or as an idea with vague wording, forget it. You won't have a belief to change.

I keep saying you 'must' and you 'have to.' You must and you have to only **IF** you take the business of changing your old, destructive beliefs seriously. If you don't take the work seriously, you won't change any beliefs at all.

Once you have the old belief **written down** in front of you, you must write down a new, constructive belief that has more meaning for you now, at this point in your life, than the old one does. The wording of the new belief has just as much importance as the wording of the old belief.

Incidentally, merely negating the old belief won't work at all. For example, let's assume that you had a destructive, old core belief that sounded something like, "Perfection can exist in reality." You cannot create a 'new' belief by simply negating the old one. If you did, it would sound like this: "I do not believe that perfection can exist in reality." **That does not express a 'new' belief about perfection, it merely creates a new belief about the old belief.** It says that "I now believe that my old belief about perfection no longer has any significance for me."

The truly new belief has to focus on perfection, not upon my old belief **about** perfection.

If you had an old core belief that said, "My life has no value," you couldn't create a legitimate new belief by saying that, " I no longer believe that my life has no value."

How to Change Your Beliefs

You cannot replace, "Everybody has to like me" with "I do not believe that everybody has to like me." You cannot replace, "No one must ever cause me pain" with "I do not believe that no one must cause me pain." You get the point.

No evidence whatsoever exists in reality for the notion that you can record over the old tapes of your old beliefs. No amount of hypnosis, incantation or wishful thinking will blank them out once they have dropped into your below conscious mind. Those old tapes will remain with you for the rest of your life. They may show up in your dreams or possibly in some occasional flashes of waking memory. Suffering a rare, passing whiff of an old belief once in a while, over the remaining years of your life, sounds a lot better, and more constructive, than **acting on** those old beliefs for the rest of your life. You can not erase the tapes of your old beliefs but fortunately you can make new tapes of new beliefs and play them louder by acting on them.

I use the example of a large audio cassette tape player, a 'boom box,' if you will, that plays the old beliefs in our head. Picture each old belief stored on a shelf with a number under each belief. Our belief about 'the most important thing I know' sits in position number one. Our belief about perfection sits in position number two. Our belief about our definition of love sits in position number three. After that, the remaining positions hold different, individually determined beliefs.

Your objective, should you choose to accept the challenge, requires you to evaluate every significant situation you find yourself in and determine which core beliefs you hear playing in your head. You must try to identify the exact nature of the situation in which you find yourself and the number of the belief, or beliefs, playing in the background.

For example, every time you find yourself in the situation of 'having a relationship,' what core beliefs do you start acting on? Perhaps your number four old belief tells you that, "I must always keep other people happy." When you hear that one playing, recog-

An Ultimate Truth

nize its reality and say something to yourself like, "Well, there goes old number four again!"

After you have created a new belief to offset old belief number four, you will have the power to add an important next step to the process that previously would have ended when you said, "Well, there goes old number four again."

With a new belief, taken from a different mental shelf which holds all your new beliefs, you can say to your Self, "Now I'll play my new tape number four-A." Four-A may sound like, "I have to keep my Self happy first, other people second."

Visualize two tape players in every situation you find yourself in, one playing the old tape created in your childhood and the other one playing the new tape you recently created. In effect, by acting on the new belief, you can turn up the volume on the new tape. In that way it can overwhelm the old tape over time.

Remember, your old beliefs took a lifetime to become convictions. They became convictions because you acted on them year after year after year. It will take some time acting on the new beliefs to make them yours. If you act on your new belief every time a situation warrants it, you will eventually overwhelm the old tape, depending of course upon how often you get into that situation and depending upon how often you activate the new belief you created once you find your Self in the situation.

Since repetition turns beliefs into convictions, I recommend that you pick situations to start with that occur fairly often.

Then identify the old belief, or beliefs, that a particular situation activates. That way you will have numerous opportunities to play the new tape in your head and to turn up the volume by acting on it. "There goes old tape number seven again, I'd better pull new belief tape number seven-A off the new tape shelf and turn up the volume by acting on it."

I suggest that you pick as many simple, frequently occurring situations as you can to start with. Don't tackle the biggest

How to Change Your Beliefs

issues in your life first. I apologize in advance for the cliché but you have to crawl before you can walk or run.

Beware of perfectionistic old beliefs that might lead you to want to take on the most difficult situation in your life first.

Beware also of the all or nothing, black or white dysfunctional thinking that might lead you to quit if you don't score a complete success the first time you try this. Even one-on-one with a coach, it takes time.

I ask you to consider just how much power this process places in your hands. Your beliefs run your life. They determine all your choices, therefore they determine all your voluntary actions, and, they determine virtually all of your emotions. They determine what you will perceive as stressful.

Your old beliefs, the ones that run your life today, came from other people in another time; and most of them probably no longer have any validity for the person you have become. Old beliefs that got you through a traumatic and dysfunctional childhood will, if retained, make your adult life a painful, miserable and isolated experience.

This good news, this very good news, says that you can voluntarily create your own functional, healthy beliefs **for the very first time**. Last time, when you were a child, other people created beliefs for you. You can do it on purpose this time, for your Self. You can create new beliefs that will overwhelm and eventually replace your dysfunctional old beliefs. For the first time in your life, your beliefs can support and serve the constructive Self interests of your **today and tomorrow**, rather than the yesterdays of your dysfunctional past.

PART THREE

58

Dangerous Thinking

In the last part of the last chapter I advised you to beware of dysfunctional, black-and-white thinking. I would like to warn you about some additional thought patterns that characterize a dysfunctional state of mind. For example, you will know that you suffer from intellectual dysfunction:

- when you draw broad, sweeping conclusions from very little evidence. If someone frowns at you, you will conclude that the person hates you and wishes to see you dead from a horrible, disfiguring disease.
- when you jump to a conclusion after having only one experience. If you fail at something once, you conclude that you will never, ever succeed at anything again.
- when you blow up a very, very remote possibility into a certainty. You know, beyond any doubt, that the airplane carrying you will crash in a horrible fireball and kill everyone on board.
- when you create disasters that supposedly will occur if you don't get what you want. "Give me that promotion/ marry me/tell me you love me/ or I will kill myself."
- when you know you can read other people's minds. "I know the boss really hates me."
- when you constantly compare yourself to others, and always come out better or worse.
- when you believe that everything that goes wrong in your life will result in a disaster, calamity and the end of the world as you know it.

An Ultimate Truth

- when you believe that your emotions automatically express profound truth for the rest of the world. If you feel it, everyone else must feel it too.

- when you believe that everyone else on earth shares your beliefs.

- when you lean way back to avoid falling on your face. You exaggerate reality in a direction opposite the thing you fear. You overwhelm people you hate with kindness.

- when you can't express your feelings directly. You kick the dog or yell at your partner because you can't allow yourself to yell at your boss.

- when you focus on tiny little inconsequential things to avoid facing large and unpleasant realities.

- when you talk in triangles. You tell your child to give your partner messages for you. You talk to your partner through your dog, your cat or your parakeet.

- when you really hate something you see in another person because you can't accept the same thing in yourself. Because you have repressed it, you can't stand to see it appear in someone else.

- when you put your own negative, destructive behaviors onto the back of some other person or thing in order to avoid responsibility. "The devil made me do it."

- when you don't like your Self and therefore believe that nobody else likes you either.

- when someone accuses you of doing something destructive and you blindly and automatically accuse them of doing the same thing even though you have no evidence for your accusation.

- when you start stealing characteristics from your heroes. You see something you like in another person and decide that you have it too, even though you don't.

Dangerous Thinking

- when you start defining your identity by your possessions.
- when you start turning your fantasies and your wishes into indisputable facts of reality. For example, when you believe that words spoken with sincerity automatically deliver truth.
- when you start using your intelligence to deny truth. You define negatives as positives simply because you wish it so.
- when you tune out of reality now or if you have ever tuned out of it in the past. You can disconnect your Self from past or present emotions; thoughts and images; emotions only; thoughts only; images only; or any awareness of anything. You can create great gaps in your memories. Sometimes you can blank out years of your life at a time.
- when you start playing, "If only" games in your head. If only I had the right job/partner/smile/figure/hair/skin/sex or car/friends/connections etc. I would experience happiness.
- when you feel compelled to create fantasies about your parents in order to redeem and salvage a dysfunctional past; when you feel the need to distract your Self from seeing your childhood as a total waste.
- when you believe that you must control everything and everyone around you to prevent it and them from hurting you.

When it comes to dysfunctional thinking, I have heard it said that neurotics build castles in the sky because they *fear* reality. Psychotics, on the other hand, *deny* reality, so they move right into the castles and set up housekeeping. Meanwhile, people in the mental health field collect the rent. If you have heard this story before, my apologies.

Intellectual dysfunction, as expressed by these examples, and others, can alert you to the need for help. Thinking about *how* you think probably does not rate high on your list of personal priorities but I can promise you that an early awareness of the

An Ultimate Truth

dysfunctional nature of your own thoughts can help head off a later disaster.

59

Delivering Information

Physical, Intellectual, emotional and spiritual dysfunction affects our ability to communicate in a healthy way with other people.

I define communications in a way that I believe makes it acceptable to the majority of us. I suggest that we define communications as a **transfer of information** between living people. This definition requires the presence of at least one living, viable consciousness in the loop. One person gives off information, in many different ways, and another person receives that information. That person can only receive the other person's information if they have engaged their consciousness and their senses in order to pick it up. One person, alone, may transmit a million messages to their environment but if no other human shares that same environment, communication can not occur. Communication, in the human sense, requires both a sender and a receiver. Give a speech to an empty room and you only transmit information to the walls, you do not 'communicate' with those walls. You only communicate if you have a living, conscious person with you in that otherwise empty room.

A clock on the wall transmitting information does not qualify as a communicator until a living consciousness receives and registers the information transmitted by the clock. Two clocks on the same wall can not 'communicate' with each other since no living consciousness receives any information.

The most important thing I can tell you about human communication involves the amount of information we deliver to our environment. **We deliver some kind of information to our environment 100% of the time.** No moment passes in which we do not transmit **some** kind of information to our surroundings or to the people in those surroundings.

An Ultimate Truth

My experience has shown that we typically only spend about 5% of our waking time aware of what we transmit. That means that about 95% of the time we have no clue as to the nature or the amount of the information we present to those around us.

We transmit information through the meanings of our words, the way we use those words and our body movements, known as 'body language.' By now, you must have seen the percentages, sometime in your life, which describe how we get our direct, sensory information from people: 55% from body language, 38% from the way words and combinations of words sound and 7% from the meaning of the actual spoken words themselves. I believe these percentages came from a study done at the University of Pennsylvania in 1970. On the phone, in my experience, about 80% of the information comes from the way words sound and about 20% comes from the meaning of the words themselves. Without direct viewing, word presentation supplants body language as our greatest source of information.

An observer could watch us and get *some* kind of information from us during every second of the time spent observing. You constantly transmit information. It only requires the presence of another person, receiving your transmission, to convert it from a transmission into a communication. Information transferred to, and received by, another living person becomes a communication.

Even when we sleep, we transmit tremendous amounts of information to our surroundings. It merely requires an observer to turn those transmissions into communications: into information transferred from you to him or her. You can have some fun if you attempt to identify all the information available to the observer of a sleeping person.

Even a corpse communicates a great deal of information to an interested observer: approximate height, weight, gender and age; ethnicity, color of skin; color of hair; presence or absence of hair; possibly the manner of death; possibly the disfigurements of a fatal disease. A corpse would communicate vast amounts of important information to an interested forensic pathologist.

Delivering Information

You transfer (communicate) information to your surroundings 100% of your time, living or dead, awake or asleep. I suggested that during 95% of our waking time, most of us have no idea what we have just communicated or how we have communicated it. That means that other people will have more knowledge about what we just did or said than we do. They will have power over us because of that. This ties in directly with our earlier discussions concerning beliefs and other people's ability to identify our beliefs merely by observing them.

Raise your awareness of what you communicate and you increase your personal power by exactly that much. You will also remove the power other people have over you by that same amount. If you increased your awareness from 5% to 10%, you would double your existing personal power. Obviously you could never reach a 100% awareness of what you communicate because then you would spend all your time watching your Self and none of your time doing anything. I train my clients to practice a kind of rolling, ongoing Self awareness that operates constantly. A portion of every moment gets devoted to some level of objective Self awareness. I get them to include this as part of their vigilance, their ongoing Self maintenance.

I respectfully ask you to remember that you communicate something to someone **all** of the time you share space with them. You don't have to say one word to communicate volumes through body language. You can say just one word in various ways and communicate entirely different meanings. Try saying the word 'honey' in as many different ways as you can to a group of your friends and keep track of all the different messages you deliver, depending on your intonation, volume and emphasis. Consider how many possibilities exist for miscommunications when we use entire sentences, made up of many words. Try to raise your awareness of how much information you constantly transfer, by different delivery systems, to every observer. The higher your awareness of what you transmit and how you transmit it, the greater your personal power.

An Ultimate Truth

In practical terms, for daily living, I recommend that you constantly hear a different, soft, little voice in each ear. In one ear I suggest that you hear the statement, "100%" over and over. This of course refers to the fact that you communicate (transmit) something to your environment during 100% of your reality. In the other ear I suggest that you hear, "More than half" over and over. This refers to the 55% of your total transfer of information that occurs as a result of your body language. Actually, if you add up the 55% from body language and the 38% from the way we deliver our words, 93% of our total communications to another person have nothing whatsoever to do with the actual meanings of the actual words we use. We could speak our language poorly and only obscure 7% of the total information we transmit. Pre-language babies do a terrific job of this. We may not understand one sound they make but we certainly get their message from the way they deliver those sounds and their body language during the delivery.

Since we communicate something to our environment 100% of the time, it becomes our challenge to see how much awareness we can have of what we deliver. As I said, a 10% awareness would probably double what most people have now.

60
Bursting The Bubble

Another impediment to communicating with other people shows up when we try to get someone's attention. We all live in a bubble, with all of our problems, concerns, fears and preoccupations. Just dealing with all our cares requires most of our concentration. We generally prefer to stay in our bubble with the known, rather than to venture outside into the unknown.

Actually, we can get someone's attention very easily. We can get them to come out of their bubble very simply. Raising your voice just about always does it. Lowering your voice suddenly to a whisper can also do it. Sit down when others stand or stand when others sit. Start taking off your clothes in a crowded public place. Just starting, without finishing, will get you all kinds of attention.

The problem occurs after we get someone out of their bubble, by any means. Everyone comes out with a big sign around their neck that says, "Give me a reason to stay out here!" If we don't, they pop right back in. **Getting people to come out of their bubble takes no great effort: keeping them out does.**

We have to offer something of value to **them**, not to us. We must offer them a win-win proposition in order to keep their attention. In aggressive behavior, I win and you lose. In passive behavior, you win and I lose. In assertive behavior, we both win. You may have heard all this before. What you may never have heard before however defines the behavior in which we both lose. I want to give credit to one of my former colleagues, V. Havar, Ph.D., for the term 'reactive' behavior which, as far as I know, she originated. When someone else speaks, if we only react to what they say and then focus exclusively on **our** rebuttal rather than on **their** message, we have engaged in reactive behavior. Since we spend all our time together just reacting to each other, we both lose

An Ultimate Truth

an opportunity for any kind of meaningful dialogue during the transaction.

Win-win means that I have to discover something you value and tie it to what I want and value. If I want your help, you probably will not want to give it to me unless you can see something of value for your Self in the act of helping me.

In order to discover anything about someone else, we have to shut up and listen to them.

We can't learn anything about someone else if we only hear our own voice. That goes for our own voice in our head too. We can drown out someone else's spoken words by turning up the volume of our own voice, in our own thoughts, in our own heads. That qualifies as a distractive drug of choice if we choose to do it frequently enough. It could also qualify as trophy polishing as it sets up defenses against insight and assures us that we will suffer due to our ignorance of other people's words.

A great way to discover what other people want requires us to simply ask them. "I need your help and I want to know what I can do to obtain it." Most people will not snap back into their bubble after an offer like that.

61

Too Much Empathy

Communicating in two directions requires us to get someone else's attention and then to hold it. Asking them what we can do to keep their attention works.

Seeing reality through their eyes will also help us to understand what they need or want. Seeing through other people's eyes fits the definition of 'empathy.' I believe that empathy can get us into a lot of trouble if we use the incorrect definition of the concept.

For example, suppose you want to sell another person a 'no' and they want to sell you a 'yes.' What happens if you become so successfully empathetic that you become 100% empathetic with that other person? Right, you will become them. You will become **sympathetic**, which means that you will see reality exactly the same way they do. You will lose your point of view if you become 100% empathetic with them. You will give up trying to sell them a 'no' and accept their 'yes' without reservation.

The common and, in my opinion, destructive definition of empathy focuses exclusively on **what** the other person thinks and feels. The common definition requires you walk a mile in their shoes and see the world through their eyes in order to experience their reality.

I recommend a different definition of empathy. I suggest that you focus more on **how** they think rather than on **what** they think. Having a healthier definition of empathy will mean that you try to empathize with, to understand, their thought **process** itself, rather than just the output of that process.

If you focus primarily on how they think rather than what they think, you will never fall into the trap of losing your point of view.

An Ultimate Truth

Once you understand their thought *process*, you can fully comprehend their point of view and, at the same time, feel free to disagree with them without running the risk of compromising your own position.

62

Differences of Opinion

If we have healthy intellectual and emotional boundaries we will inevitably disagree with people occasionally. We will have to say 'no' and we may have to say it very emphatically to get their attention.

Arguing means discussing a topic from two or more points of view. Healthy arguing keeps to the issues involved and does not degenerate into personal attacks on the character of the opposing party.

We cannot argue about opinions. If I have a painting on the wall of my office, and I like it, my client may very well hate it. We have different opinions about the painting, period. If either one of us decided to try to change the opinion of the other and convince them that they held a wrong opinion, we would waste our time and energy and only antagonize the other person.

A differing opinion does not automatically qualify as a wrong opinion. Only a dysfunctional, fantasy based belief could take such an absurd position. For example, if I believed that, "All opinions that differ from mine automatically become wrong opinions," I would spend most of my life in conflict.

You and I both know people who fit this profile exactly, and they **do** spend most of their life in conflict.

Now, if two art critics decided to evaluate my painting on the wall, and both critics had about the same training in graphic arts, the same experience as professional artists themselves and the same amount of experience as critics, they could argue reasonably for hours over the technical merits of the painting. They could argue for or against the success or failure of the artist in terms of perspective, focal point, composition, subject matter, abstract equivalents, brush technique, use of colors etc.. They could try to convince each other that they held a 'wrong' opinion, based upon

An Ultimate Truth

the quantifiable, objective reality of the work itself. Arguments based upon facts reflect healthy disagreements. **Arguments based upon opinions reflect dysfunctional beliefs.**

One of the most common, argument stopping statements, used by just about everybody, sounds something like this: "Well, anything can happen. Everything falls into the realm of possibility doesn't it?" Does it?

If you occasionally become the victim of someone who uses a statement like that to have the last word in an argument, and if you **can** imagine anything as possible, I want to offer you another statement that means **exactly** the same thing; but you will probably not agree with it.

If you can imagine **anything as possible**, you should have no trouble imagining **nothing as impossible**. Yet, you will. You will not feel comfortable with the second statement, even though it has precisely the same meaning as the first. You can easily visualize truly impossible things in reality.

I offer you this example to demonstrate that even supposedly unassailable arguments have their flaws and defects.

With healthy boundaries in place, we can reasonably and rationally disagree with any statement, position or concept that attempts to violate our intellectual or emotional space.

A functional person has created a solid place to stand; a 'high ground' from which he or she can take on reality in a fair fight.

You have to establish an ongoing maintenance program to take care of the high ground you have worked so hard to earn. Like any structure you build, you have to look after it regularly or it will crumble and decay. The window through which you view reality must get a regular cleaning, especially considering how hard you had to work to scrape off the years of dysfunctional garbage in the first place.

One component of our lifelong process of 'vigilance' requires us to disagree with anything that poses a threat to our high

Differences of Opinion

ground, to any of the four aspects of our Self, and to our ability to defend, protect, develop and celebrate our Self at all times. The other part involves monitoring our choices and our emotions. I will address that second part of vigilance in the last chapter.

An Ultimate Truth

63

The Risks of Forgiveness

You must defend your Self against one particularly insidious form of extortion: the demand that you forgive your abusers.

By forgiveness I mean unconditionally absolving the abuser of responsibility for your pain and suffering. Forget it. It won't work. I have had numerous clients who tried to absolve their abusers and it never, ever worked. Generally, it made matters worse, not better.

This type of unconditional, unilateral forgiveness springs from the notion that every parent does the best they know how to do. Therefore, they shouldn't receive any blame for destroying their kid's life because of their lack of parenting skills, common sense or because of an addiction.

In a business or a government, we can put corporate officers or political figures in jail for breaking laws but not for incompetence, poor judgment or stupidity.

The same applies to parents. Because they abused their children due to a lack of knowledge or due to the pain of their own unresolved issues, the majority stay out of jail. If they go too far in their abuse of course, they won't.

Breaking laws make parents accountable. Breaking spirits and hearts often leaves them untouched and unaccountable.

The concept of blame gives most people a headache. When do we blame, when do we not?

If our parents belonged to a cult that taught them to abuse their children every day, then the abuse would have occurred on purpose. Purposeful behavior deserves blame. If we had parents who, for any reason whatsoever intentionally abused us, cult or not, they deserve all the blame we, and the law, can heap upon them.

An Ultimate Truth

On the other hand, most parents abused their children unintentionally, out of their own dysfunction. They simply had no training for the most difficult job on earth. The best they knew to do turned into the worst thing for their kids. **Their** best fell miles short of **the** best. I know that when I first became a parent, many years ago, I made a ton of mistakes out of ignorance.

Without going into a long dissertation on parenting, at least in this book, let me briefly state the basic, fundamental duties of parents. First, they have to meet the physical needs of their child, like food, clothing and shelter. Second, they have to make sure that the child doesn't suffer physical damage. Third, they have to satisfy the child's requirements for love, acceptance, attention and recognition. Fourth, they have to look after the child's emotional health. Fifth, they have to provide the intellect of the child with a map of acceptable behaviors.

A parents' dysfunction wipes out their ability to accomplish the duties on this list from the bottom up. Mild dysfunction eliminates duty number five and progressively severe dysfunction will eventually eliminate the rest of them. For example, if an individual's own dysfunction has progressed to the point where they can't even meet their own physical needs, they certainly won't have the capacity to provide for any of the child's needs.

In my not too humble opinion, I believe that parenting should require a license independent of a marriage license. Then, people could at least receive some instruction on how to perform the world's most difficult task before the fact, not after it. The biological ability to reproduce puts parents into a position of responsibility for creating and **sustaining** a new life. Dysfunction guarantees irresponsibility towards that new life. A new life may not survive such irresponsibility or, if it does, it may do so with more emotional, and possibly physical, scar tissue than healthy tissue.

If we can only blame people for things they do on purpose, what can we do with people who have hurt us unintentionally? **We can hold them accountable.** The person, or persons, who caused

The Risks of Forgiveness

you physical, intellectual, emotional and spiritual pain carry a full load of responsibility for having done so.

If you remember my example from a previous chapter on anger, when someone bumps into you and causes you pain, it doesn't matter whether they did it accidentally or on purpose. It still hurts. You hold them accountable for your pain. They caused it. No one else caused it, they did. Even if you love the person who caused you the pain, and they did it accidentally, **you still hurt**. **That person caused your pain.**

They bear responsibility for having caused you to suffer, irrespective of whether they did it purposefully or not. You can not absolve someone of the truth. You dare not intentionally choose to replace a reality with a fantasy or you will lose your functionality.

Denying reality will only get you into trouble. You can choose to accept the reality that your parents did the best they could and didn't really **try** to make your life a painful, tormented experience. If you do, you can intellectually understand how their dysfunction got passed on to you. You can choose to eliminate the need to avenge your Self. You can choose to give up any thoughts of revenge and recognize the victim status of your parents. Remember, they may have come out of a more dysfunctional, screwed up family system than you did.

However, they may have committed an unpardonable act. Unfortunately you will probably never know if they did or not. I mention it to warn **you** so that at least you will not do this terrible thing. Suppose a parent **un**intentionally abuses a child out of their own ignorance and dysfunction. The first time it happens, we could perhaps absolve them of their responsibility due to their own dysfunction, maybe. What about the second time it happens? I remember a particular client's experience with this as a very young child. Her father initially put up an emotional wall so that he would never have to show her any direct evidence of his love and affection. He had some **big** problems with unresolved emotional issues. She remembered failing to scale his wall in the beginning, but eventually she got very close to the top. You know what he did then? Right. He raised the wall. He added some bricks to the top. His own unresolved emotional issues caused him to build the walls in the first place. What about the **second** place? He might get off the hook for doing what he did the first time but what motivated him to build them higher the second time? His motivation came from the discovery that what he did the first time worked like a charm. It kept the kid away from him emotionally the first time he did it. Why not do it again? He unintentionally built the wall the first time out of ignorance. He **intentionally** added bricks to it the second time. That second ruthless act deserves no absolution or pardon.

Parents generally have no idea how much damage they have done to their children even when faced with overwhelming evidence of suicides, addictions and every kind of misery and suffering a person could experience. Their own dysfunction provides a protective wall of defense against any insight or understanding of the pain they have inflicted. I have seen this tragic reality repeated over and over, in family after family. Children often have to divorce themselves from their mothers and fathers in order to protect their own sanity from the dysfunction of their parents. At best, as the years go by, the children can only allow themselves very limited contact with these parents to minimize the risk of further contamination. The parents will never understand why their own children avoid them since they would only deny the truth if they heard it. It makes for some very sad and painful situations.

One of the more sorrowful situations in my client files occurred after a divorced, single, male parent married a new spouse admittedly, among other reasons, to make up for his own personal shortcomings in child rearing. He selected his new wife partly to get off the hook as a parent. His choice caused some horrendous consequences for his son in later years. He made the original choice for his own sake, not the kid's. The best thing for him resulted in the worst experience for the boy. The woman he chose made the life of his child a pit of despair which later developed into profound dysfunction for him as an adult. When that adult first

The Risks of Forgiveness

came to me as a client, he had already made numerous attempts at suicide. To this day, after many years, that father can't understand why his son wants nothing to do with his stepmother and won't play along with his father's fantasy that his wife walks on water. To the father, she does. To the son, she definitely doesn't.

If you absolve abusers of responsibility for your pain, you in effect say that the abuse never happened. I had a female client who came under great pressure from her church, her brothers and her sisters to 'forgive' an uncle who had sexually abused her. She couldn't do it. As she and I talked, her fury and her rage emerged towards the abusing relative. She also directed a great deal of anger at those who had encouraged her to forgive the one who had violated her as a child. **She said that if she forgave the perpetrator, in order to satisfy her church and family, it would seem to others as if, in her mind, the event had never occurred.** And, to her great credit, she did not want to deny reality, even one as heinous and repugnant as the one she had experienced.

I had another client who tried to forgive and failed. His motivation to do so came from his religious leader. After he had tried to forgive and failed, over and over again, he told me that he felt ashamed, stupid, inadequate, humiliated, weak and victimized yet again. When he returned to his 'spiritual' advisor for comfort, he learned that, according to the advisor, he had failed because he 'didn't have enough faith.' With those words, his already fragile state collapsed. He attempted suicide.

We must fully express our emotional outrage over abuse, if only to our Selves. When the abuse originally occurred, we repressed our healthy emotional reactions to avoid more abuse. **It must come out.** If we intellectually choose to forgive our abusers, and the repressed emotions have not yet found release, we will wind up hating and destroying our Self as a substitute for expressing our outrage at the real thing.

We can intellectually give up the need for revenge but absolving someone of their responsibility for our pain can only occur after something else happens first.

An Ultimate Truth

Hundreds of books sit on the shelves of people who want help dealing with the subject of confronting abusive parents. I won't reinvent the wheel but I will sum up the basics. First, when confronted, 99% of parents deny that anything ever happened. Second, they deny the reality of their child's memories. Third, they deny that anything they may have done could have hurt the child.

The thing that absolutely, positively **has** to happen before any forgiveness can occur seems like an impossibility. Parents have to **deserve** our forgiveness. I told you it would seem impossible. They can earn it by **acknowledging what they did to us, accepting our memories as real and acknowledging that what they did hurt us.**

If anyone ever urges you to 'forgive and forget' the abuse you suffered in the past, I hope you interpret their advice correctly.

If you choose to forgive, without the abuser having earned your forgiveness, you will guarantee that you remain a victim of that person for the rest of your days.

If you choose to forget, to deny reality, you deprive yourself of the kind of memories that you will need to motivate the protective aspect of your vigilance in the future.

If you create a fantasy to live in that contains no memory of past abuse, you will have no reason to set healthy boundaries in the future to protect your Self from further victimization. Since you will not remember that you have anything to fear and since you will, therefore, have no anger in your fantasy to activate protective boundaries, why should you bother with them?

You won't, and you will suffer accordingly.

Let me give you a glimpse of the kind of intellectual and emotional programming a survivor of abuse has to overcome before they can finally reach the stage where they can begin to consider confronting their abuser. Incidentally, the intensity of abuse has little significance. So- called 'mild' abuse can destroy a life just as completely as 'severe' abuse. The survivor has to face facts and feelings that they have buried for years. The outrage that

The Risks of Forgiveness

has never had an outlet has to get permission to come to the surface for the first time. They have to suffer the burning, searing pain of raw emotions never before acknowledged. And friends, family members or religious advisors may ask this person to 'forgive and forget' at this point.

To underscore the difficulty of forgiveness, I want to offer you some true, real life examples of the kind of programming that incest survivors often suffer from during their childhood. The incest offender, in this case a male, frequently threatens the victim by saying that, "If you tell, I'll cut off your head; I'll slash you with my belt until your skin falls off in shreds; your mother will get a horrible disease and die; people will think you have gone crazy and put you in an asylum with all the other sick, crazy people; everybody will know you lie; your mother will get furious and hate both of us; I will always hate you; they will throw your mother and me in jail and you won't get fed; I will dump you in the garbage." or, "I will put the handle of this long, sharp knife in you and if you ever tell, I will turn it around."

You, or anyone else, will not help this person, in any way, by telling them to 'forgive and forget.'

An Ultimate Truth

64

Letting It Out

    I would like to give you some practical advice on how to express anger in a healthy, constructive way. Present anger can reach way back into our early life and allow our past anger to come roaring up to the surface of our awareness. We tend to let the accumulation of present angers add up until we can no longer prevent their expression. Then, they erupt with such violence and depth that they hook into our repressed, past anger and we go berserk. The way to prevent this from constantly recurring requires us to vent the present angers safely and expeditiously, before the day ends. If we can do that, we can stop the repression/explosion/repression/explosion cycle. How do we do that?

    If you make time for doing anything during the day, like eating or sleeping or working or loving, you can include some time for expressing current anger. You need food, sleep, money and love; and you need a time to vent. Fail to meet any one of these needs and you can cause your Self serious harm, even death. You can't survive for long without food, sleep, economic resources, love or emotional expression. Plan time to express emotions if survival interests you.

    Expressing anger on purpose, in a safe, intentional, and constructive way, makes more sense to a functional person than stuffing emotions for days or weeks at a time and then blowing up in the wrong place, at the wrong time, with the wrong person.

    Most people react to the idea of planning for anger with the statement, "But what if I don't happen to feel angry when I have the opportunity to vent?"

    Emotions aggressively look for openings in the walls you have built around them. They may not come charging through the breach the first time you sit down to feel mad, but eventually they will see the light and you may find them there waiting for you the next time you try it.

If you wait until you feel angry, you have waited too long. When you already feel angry, you won't plan ahead to do anything healthy. You won't express your feelings in a safe and constructive way and you will run the risk of tapping into your repressed emotions and doing, or saying, something Self destructive.

Think of planning for anger as preventive maintenance for your mental (and physical) health. You hopefully change the oil in your car **before** the engine seizes up, not after. You put in anti-freeze **before** the temperature drops to forty degrees below zero, not after your engine block has split. You put on your best suit **before** the job interview, not after you get home. You get dental check ups and cleanings **now** so that you will not have to get drilled later. You tell someone you love them **now** in case you don't ever get the chance to say it later.

Given the opportunity, today's suppressed angers will emerge in full force. Just a reminder, even though I have said this to you before, suppression refers to the short term, shallow burial of emotions. Repression refers to a deep, long term burial. Your suppressed emotions may not leap out at you the first time, or even the second or third time you try. Eventually they will.

You don't have to do anything special to set the stage for experiencing today's present, suppressed anger. I have had many clients do a terrific job while driving their car. They close the windows and yell their heads off. In a loud voice, they call their sources of anger and frustration foul names. Drivers of other cars who happen to look at them see their mouth moving and assume they caught them in the act of singing. No one can hear them. They achieve a tremendously therapeutic benefit without cost.

Most people benefit from writing down all the things they fear saying directly. Some can't do this, but the majority can, and do. One client left my office announcing his intention to write at home on his computer terminal. I had to chase after him to say that I wanted him to write by hand. Nothing beats the cathartic power

Letting It Out

of grabbing a writing instrument, physically attacking a piece of paper and giving form to things you have never said before.

Other clients break pencils. Some move on to break one quarter inch diameter dowel rods, by the dozens. I have clients all over the country beating on dead trees in the woods with sticks.

Pillow bashing helps. You can buy padded foam bats from a catalogue. I had a client who demolished a bean bag chair with a cane. I never knew so many little plastic pellets came in those things.

By now you have to see the pattern in all this. Bashing, beating, hitting, yelling, breaking, all express aggressive, violent behavior, albeit in a controlled environment. Walking hard by digging in your heels qualifies as violent behavior too, so it doesn't have to always reflect major physical activity. Unfortunately, violence has to play a big part in expressing buried anger. I say unfortunately because I don't personally like that reality. I accept it as real of course but I don't like it. My fantasies prefer to see buried anger dissipated intellectually, not by crude, sweaty physical exertion. So much for my fantasies. Anger makes us sweat and yell and want to break things. I don't like that reality but nobody ever checked with me first. Humans become 'physically engaged' when they express anger. **The way to release unexpressed, buried anger requires the physical action we initially denied our Selves.** We can not get away with merely **saying** that we feel angry, with no energy, intensity, depth, volume or passion in our voice. That kind of behavior identifies people with major dysfunctions immediately. Their words and the emotions behind those words just don't match.

My favorite exercise only requires you to sit in a chair next to a bed holding a wooden stick in your hand. Broom handles work very well, without the sweeping part. Sit in the chair and rest the end of the stick on the bed. **Do not try to feel anger!** Get used to the idea that you don't **have** to feel anything. Begin to tap the stick on the bed. You still don't have to feel anything. Tap the stick some more. Try to tap it a little harder. Don't feel anything. Keep on bouncing the stick off the mattress. One of two things will happen.

An Ultimate Truth

First, you might get bored and fall asleep with the wooden stick in your hand or second, you might start to feel something. In the beginning of this process, it could go either way. Give it time and try it repeatedly.

It always impresses me how many people this simple process helps. Some few never experience any emotions bubbling up at all during the exercise. Another few go wild and wind up beating their mattress to death. The majority eventually feel little bubbles of anger pop and sputter in their gut. You must continue trying **not** to feel anything in the beginning. You must present a neutral stage for your emotions to play upon.

Physical activity can lead to emotional activity. The next time you feel like misery personified, force yourself to smile while looking in a mirror. Don't try to feel happy, just force the muscles of your face into some contorted expression that could, with imagination, represent a smile. Do this for at least five minutes. Chemical changes will occur during those five minutes, both in your body and in your brain, that will provide a mild, mood elevating sensation. You won't go leaping around the room in hysterical joy and laughter but you will probably experience a small emotional change for the better. Multiply this effect by all the rest of the muscle groups in your whole body and you create some significant and powerful possibilities for your Self, emotionally.

Try this. Sit in a chair and hunch over into a fetal position with your elbows on your knees and your hands over your eyes. Make your face express misery with a scowl and a frown. Now try to say, "I FEEL TERRIFIC!" and mean it.

Or, try this. Stand on a mountain top or at the edge of the ocean and raise your hands up over your head. Look upwards towards the sun with a huge smile on your face and try to say, "I FEEL TERRIBLE! and mean it.

Powerful connections weld mind and body together. Each can lead the other, depending on circumstances. Tapping a stick on a mattress can lead emotions of anger to the surface. In different circumstances, the emotion of anger could easily lead someone to

Letting It Out

tap a stick, real hard, on just about anything, or anyone, they can reach.

Many years ago, a female client got this assignment from me and at our next session she appeared wearing a bandage on her forehead and a smile on her face. She and I had worked together for quite a while on surfacing some deeply buried and elusive repressed emotions. She had done exactly what I had asked her to do and she sat by the bed with a stick. She tapped and waited. Nothing. She repeated the process over and over to no avail. Still nothing. She quit for the day. She tried again the next day. Still nothing. Third day, the same. By the fourth day she had given up but tried again anyway. Tap, tap, tap. Wham! Anger boiled up out of her like a volcano. She went from tapping to beating and from anger to rage in a matter of seconds. She got up from the chair. She stood and flailed away at the bed. She had the stature of a large, mature, powerful person. She got a little wild. The stick bounced off a bedside lamp and ricocheted to the wall and then to her head. She briefly sat down, slightly dazed with a lump on her forehead. She recovered and went at it again. She pounded that mattress until her arms couldn't move any longer and she couldn't catch her breath. Then she stopped and cried for six straight hours.

Something beyond words and beyond description had dawned on her as she tapped the stick and waited for something to happen. It suddenly flashed into her memory, for the first time in over fifty years, that her grandfather had sexually abused her as a little girl, **in that same bed.**

For her, this represented a major breakthrough which enabled us build on the experience together and start to rebuild a shattered life.

I gave this same assignment to a male client. Before our next appointment, I saw him in one of the evening college classes I taught. I first saw him at a distance and waved. He waved back and kept his hand up as he walked toward me. He had a big grin on his face. When he got close enough to speak, he didn't. He pointed to the center of his hand. Still no words. I looked. I saw the

An Ultimate Truth

remains of a large blister that almost covered the palm of his hand. He still smiled. Same story. Buried emotions had broken out after he had tapped through his suppressed present anger into some very old, very powerful repressed emotions.

I don't recommend that you hit yourself over the head or blister your hands. I do recommend that you try this, or any other physical activity to liberate buried emotions of anger. It works.

A client used to occasionally allow close friends into her bedroom to look at the dents in her wall caused by the small, hard, plastic bat she had used for her exercise. She said that she always pointed to those dents with pride. Those marks represented great progress in her recovery. I believe she still has the bat and, to her great credit, uses it as needed.

I have by no means exhausted all the ways a person can physically lead emotions to consciousness. You might come up with some highly creative techniques of your own. Some day you may point to some gouges in your bedroom wall or an old blister on your hand with mixed feelings: happiness at the breakthrough it represented at the time and sadness at the pain you had to experience.

Those very same mixed feelings have profoundly effected my own life. I share the excruciating emotional pain of every client I work with. I carry the scars of every significant emotional experience we ever went through together for the rest of my life. Yet I have no words to adequately convey my pride in what they have accomplished. I can't begin to describe the overwhelming honor every client gives me when, in the grip of their pain and suffering, they choose to trust me enough to let me help.

Don't get frightened if surfacing anger brings up other emotions too. You could have anger mixed with other emotions; you could have other emotions hit you later; you could have no success bringing up anger but great success bringing up some other emotion, particularly sadness. Set the stage with neutrality, beat the mattress, and see what shows up.

65

Perchance to Dream

A brief word about dreams. I recommend that all my clients keep track of dreams that recur, dreams that show up after crises and, generally, the outstanding emotions from any dream that they can remember.

You and I both know that dreams present themselves to us symbolically, abstractly and fantastically. I have found that the feelings experienced in dreams have more significance to my clients that the fantasy dream events which precipitated them. I always ask what clients **felt** in their dream after they describe an encounter with some bizarre and ephemeral chimera. I have found that the emotions offer a solid link to our reality, while the sights, sounds, smells, tastes and touches we receive from the abstract symbols in our dreams usually fail to connect with reality.

You have experienced it. You have a dream that makes no sense whatsoever, symbolically, yet it scares you speechless. You can't even scream in the dream. How do you feel emotionally when you wake up from such a dream? Right: scared silly. Your heart races, your entire body sweats, your breath comes in gasps. What scared you in the dream may have had no lucidity at all, but you awoke with real emotions, in this world. The emotions bridge the gap between the fantasy of dreams and the reality of our wakefulness. Memories of the abstract symbols that our emotions responded to in the dream rarely bridge that gap.

Recurring dreams indicate that we consistently draw upon certain past experiences in order to deal with current problematic realities. Those past experiences may not give us the best tools for grappling with today's hassles. Drawing on them does not necessarily mean we benefit from them. I have found that, more than likely, when we did not successfully deal with our past experiences, we project those failed solutions upon similar future experiences when they come up in our dreams, perhaps in hope of finally getting them to work. They never do.

A crisis will challenge our below conscious mind to come up with creative and innovative ways to deal with shock, loss and pain through our dreams. How that part of our mind actually does it, symbolically, has a great deal of significance in as much as it demonstrates internal coping strategies at work. Internal coping strategies in dreams generally reflect external coping strategies in reality. Knowing one helps us to know the other.

Our dreams reflect our below conscious mental activity. More than anything, in my opinion, they reflect the **process** of that level of our mental activity. The 'how' of our dreams becomes much more important than the 'what'. Like empathy, understanding process has more value than understanding output. How our dreams help us to cope with reality has more practical meaning than the kind of symbols the dreams use to accomplish the coping. For that reason, my experience with clients has taught me to focus on the emotional content of dreams rather than their sensory content. We seem to get a lot more useful information that way. I believe you will too.

66

Change or Cope

I talked to you about dreams helping us to cope with current reality. I also want to give you some guidance in coping with your waking reality. In any situation, I previously recommended that you look at it as a combination of plus and minus characteristics totaling 100%. I want to offer you another overlay to apply to that situation. You will immediately see its correlation with the process of seeing reality in percentages of positive and negative.

In the 100% of any given situation or circumstance you find yourself in, you will always find a percentage of that situation that you can change. In the workplace, for example, that percentage often seems very small. In many relationships, the percentage of things that you can change often seems minuscule. On the other hand, a parent can bring about many, many changes in the situation of parenting. Also, we can constantly change our choices as to the type and duration of the entertainment we enjoy. The percentage of situations which we can change in order to distract ourselves runs very high.

So we can change little, some or much of our situations. What can we do with the remaining percentage of any situation: that portion which we can **not** change?

We cope. This model has three C's: **C**ope, **C**ircumstances and **C**hange. We cope with the circumstances we can not change.

How do we cope with what we can not change? We cope in all kinds of ways: we deny reality; we accept it but fight it; we accept it and make the best of it; we accept it unconditionally and never question it; we tolerate it until we can change it; we say that we can change it by accepting it; we accept it temporarily, for a specified length of time, then reevaluate our options. Everyone has

An Ultimate Truth

their own coping styles. Do you know yours? I guarantee that your intimate friends and partner know them very well. If you want a short cut to knowing your coping strategies, ask them. They know, even if you don't.

They may tell you that when you can't change things, you: sulk; get snappy; become morose; spend all your time and energy trying to change what you cannot; shift your pain onto others by blaming them; distract yourself into oblivion; escape into total denial.

Or, perhaps they will say that you cope by fully accepting reality, even though you don't like it, and choose to change your beliefs to either make tolerance easier or make change more likely in the future; possibly both.

They might even say that you focus all your intellectual and emotional resources on what **does** exist rather than on what **does not** exist. What a compliment!

67

Ten/eighty/ten

One of the realities most difficult to accept involves people who don't like us. Most people want to have other people like them. You do. I do. You've heard the term 'people pleaser.' It applies to externally focused individuals. A people pleaser must please everyone **but** themselves.

First, you must keep **you** happy, then you can determine who gets your attention after that. You know that by now.

I would like to offer you another model, complete with percentages, that can help keep the topic of other people liking us in perspective.

If you add up all the people you know, they will total 100%. It doesn't matter whether you know five people or five thousand, they will still total 100% if they represent **all** the people you know. How many of them do you want to like you? All of them? Some of them? A few of them? None of them?

It won't really make any difference how many of them you **want** to like you. Reality has a different idea. Reality says that of the 100% you know, only around 10% will really like you. Reality also says that about 10% of them won't like you at all. Indifference will characterize the remaining 80%.

You may not like these numbers. You may decide to move into a cave for the next ten years and reinvent your Self. You may get made over, reeducated, reoriented and redecorated during those ten years. When you come out, you won't look, smell, talk or think the same as when you went in.

Guess what? 10% of your acquaintances won't like the new you. 10% will love the new you. 80% won't care. Nothing will change. Of course you will probably have an entirely new group of acquaintances, but the percentages won't change.

An Ultimate Truth

This means that 90% of the people who know you either don't like you or don't care one way or the other. It also means that 90% of the people who know me don't like me or don't care either. I accepted this reality a long time ago. I don't like it but I accept it as real. I can't change it. Neither can you. Can you accept the reality?

10% love us, or at least like us a lot. They accept us with all our shortcomings. We don't have to try to get them to like us, they already do.

The 10% who hate us, or at least dislike us, won't accept us no matter how hard we try to get them to like us. We could spend our entire lifetime trying to convert these people and we might, possibly, slightly influence one person, maybe. Not a very good return on a lifetime investment.

The indifferent 80% might come out of their bubble, and stay out, if we give them a good enough reason. Of course, once they focus on us, they could easily wind up moving into either the 10% 'for' group of the 10% 'against' group.

These percentages obviously vary somewhat in a real world. At least when I say "ten/eighty/ten" to a client, they know what I mean. Now, you do too. Your numbers might look like 12/78/10 or 8/80/12 at any given time but the basic rule still applies.

I know that when I first heard these percentages a long time ago, and I can't remember where I first heard them, I seriously doubted their accuracy. I had to confirm them over many years of observation in practice. To my surprise, they remained constant, year after year.

I once taught a course to adult students in which I presented exactly this same material during the first half of the first class. Twenty people attended. We took a break. Eighteen people returned, two disappeared during the break. One of the students who returned astutely observed, with no prompting from me whatsoever, that at least the 10% who didn't like me had left the group,

Ten/eighty/ten

presumably to get a refund on the course, leaving only the 10% who liked me and the remaining, indifferent 80%. I had to agree.

At one time I taught people how to have more success relating to prospective buyers of their services. One young man complained bitterly that most of his prospects didn't like him. He said that since he knew everything, technically, about his service, he would just go after all those people who didn't like him and **make** them like him. He intended to convert the 90% who didn't like him or didn't care about him. He wore himself out. He spent all his time and energy trying. He failed. He almost drove himself out of his business.

I suggested that he concentrate on finding his 'natural market,' those people who automatically liked him, rather than killing himself by trying to convert those who didn't.

He did so and he became very successful. He spent his time and energy looking for **his** favorable 10% instead of wasting himself trying to convert the unconvertible 90%. He made a good living by focusing his efforts on his positive 10% **and** increasing the number of his prospects so as to always have more people to add to that favorably predisposed percentage. Once he understood ten/eighty/ten, he changed his action beliefs, his choices, his outcomes, his career and his life for the better. It empowered him. It can empower you. I challenge you to give it a try.

An Ultimate Truth

68

Unearned Guilt

We feel guilty about a lot of things. Hopefully, you will no longer feel guilty about failing to qualify as 'lovable' according to nine out of every ten people who know you.

We suffer from two kinds of guilt: earned guilt and unearned guilt. Earned guilt comes upon us when we absolutely, positively **do** screw something up. That kind of guilt indicates that we take responsibility for our choices and the outcomes of those choices. I call that healthy guilt. It shows that we accept reality as real, even though we don't like it. If I messed up, I won't like the fact that I did but I accept full responsibility for doing so. If I accept responsibility, I will feel guilty. If I feel guilty, I will have the emotional motivation necessary to try and avoid messing up again. As I said, very healthy.

Unearned guilt can cause us an enormous amount of pain. It can destroy us. I call unearned guilt very unhealthy. We experience unearned guilt when we automatically accept someone else's unproven accusation of wrongdoing. Unearned guilt finds a home when the victim voluntarily accepts it from the accuser.

I covered the topic of dysfunctional parents using unearned guilt to control their children in a previous chapter. I want to address the subject of unearned *adult* guilt in this one.

If you volunteer to take on guilt to keep somebody else happy or to pacify them, then you have volunteered to become a victim. Maybe you want to trophy polish so you need a reason to suffer. Perhaps you need to feel like a victim so that you can justify stealing other people's time, attention, compassion and concern the way every trophy polisher does.

Perhaps you take on a big ration of guilt because someone in your life uses their pain to control you. Parents do this a lot. If you believe that you have **any** responsibility for your parent's

An Ultimate Truth

happiness, you will feel unearned guilt every time they experience real or imagined unhappiness since your beliefs create your emotional state. When you choose the belief, you choose the guilt. Some parents make a career out of playing their adult children's guilt like a harp. They pluck your strings and you make the music. This only works if you have chosen to feel responsible for their state of mind.

If you believe that you carry complete responsibility for your children's happiness, you choose victimhood as well. Virtually every time your kids express unhappiness you will feel guilty. You will have chosen to live in an emotional state of constant guilt because of your belief, your **very** unrealistic belief.

If you believe that the ultimate responsibility for humanity's happiness rests on your shoulders, you will choose to exist in a perpetual state of guilt due to your certain failure.

Unearned guilt requires you to believe that you deserve something you know you don't. To feel unearned guilt, you must lie to your Self. You must tell your Self that you deserve what you know you do not. You must deny reality and you must deny your intellect and the evidence of your senses. You will only make such an absurd, dysfunctional choice when a strong emotional payoff justifies it in your mind. Trophy polishing usually provides just such a strong emotional payoff.

A strong desire for recognition as an extraordinarily humble person would do it too. I really enjoy the irony in that one.

If you wanted to impress the members of the religious organization you belong to by proving that you could never live up to an onerous theological standard, you could enjoy a satisfying and rewarding life as a guilt ridden, perpetual failure. In doing so, you would validate their belief in the inherent weakness of humanity and thereby earn their undying gratitude. You would gain an enormous emotional payoff by satisfying both the people themselves and the dictates of your religious system.

Unearned Guilt

Apropos of the above, I once had a client who believed that she existed on this earth only to suffer, and she did. She believed that her destiny required her to maintain her Self in a constant state of emotional agony. She made every choice she could in order to fulfill her own prophesy. She experienced genuine misery and genuine unhappiness. She did not trophy polish; she did not use her suffering to control other people. She answered to a higher calling. She needed to suffer in order to meet some cosmic demand, which only she perceived, that required her to represent and symbolize all of a suffering and guilt ridden humanity.

She came from a perfectionistic, demanding, unforgiving, inhuman, rigidly religious, ritualistic family system. Unearned guilt **defined** the reality of her family of origin. It destroyed any chance she might have had to enjoy even the slightest degree of happiness in her life. The instant she felt a little joy, she overwhelmed her Self with brand new guilt and remorse for having interrupted her suffering for even a moment.

Dysfunction can kill the human spirit just as effectively as the human body. Unearned guilt acts, most often, as the weapon of choice.

An Ultimate Truth

69

Say It, Don't Ask

Let me show you another weapon in the arsenal of the dysfunctional. A question. One type of question that can successfully devastate us all. A rhetorical question. A question asked for its effect rather than to gather information.

For example, "Why don't you love me any more?"

That question does not express a request for information. It expresses an emotional state of anger, pain and frustration. Rhetorical questions always do that. They hide statements we **can't** make beneath questions we **can** ask. Every rhetorical question indirectly expresses a statement we don't have the courage to make directly.

"Why don't you love me any more?" expresses an unspoken statement that would sound something like this: "Your behavior tells me that you no longer find me attractive or desirable **and** I feel lost, scared, abandoned and angry."

Rhetorical questions can easily go down in flames if someone answers them literally or answers them with another question.

To a child: "Do you have your hand in the cookie jar?" Child's answer, after quickly withdrawing the offending hand, "No!"

"Tell me **dear**, how did the car end up in the swimming pool?" Answer, "Well, I just turned left at the pump house."

"Why don't you love me any more?" Answer, "What makes you think I don't love you any more?"

"You always embarrass me when we go out." Answer, "What do you mean always?"

"You never bring me flowers any more." Answer, "Sure I do, don't you remember? I brought you flowers back in...."

An Ultimate Truth

We fear stating the truth, so we ask questions when we really want to make statements. I suggest you try making the statements you really want to make instead of disguising them as rhetorical questions. Poor boundaries prevent us from saying "No!" to unacceptable behavior. External focus causes us to worry more about other people's reactions than our own.

If you think, for example, that your partner no longer loves you, you can choose to deny that reality and bury it or you can choose to speak the truth and let the chips fall where they may. **Don't ask questions when you want to say something important to you.** If you have reason to believe that someone no longer loves you, **TELL THE TRUTH!** "I don't think you love me any more!" Always add the second part to your statements, the part that describes how you feel about what you have just stated. "I don't think you love me any more **and I feel lost, scared, abandoned and angry.**"

Don't ever omit the second part of your statement. You want to first state a fact, then state how you feel about that fact. **Facts** then **feelings**. Don't separate them when you express yourself. If you want to deliver a complete, functional, healthy and constructive message, you must state what you believe **and** also how you feel about it.

Try stating your truth in this way as often as you can. For example, "You don't treat my time with any respect. You show up late or not at all. You don't bother to call if something delays you. You expect me to do everything promptly but you don't. My time matters. When you disrespect my time you disrespect me. When you disrespect me, it makes me mad. I deserve respect and consideration and I will not tolerate this kind of behavior from anyone, much less from someone who supposedly cares about me!"

Facts and feelings: always deliver them together.

Another statement, that can help you get at someone else's truth very easily, sounds like this: "I have the impression that _____ , tell me if you agree and correct me if you don't."

Say It, Don't Ask

As before, make sure that you complete the statement by stating both halves. "I have the impression that _____" **and** "Tell me if you agree and correct me if you don't."

This statement asks for an evaluation in the most non-threatening manner possible. You make a statement and then encourage the other person to correct you. Prepare your Self to receive corrections that you may not like. You might not really want to hear someone else's truth at all. Can you accept reality even though you don't like it?

Let me give you two examples: one simple and silly, the other more real, more profound and more painful.

I have the impression that, in the English language, the letter 'i' comes before the letter 'e' except when the letter 'i' follows the letter 'c'. In that case, 'e' comes before 'i'. Please tell me if you agree and correct me if you don't.

I wish I could know what answer you came up with. I think I can safely assume that most of you probably agreed with my impression, citing our childhood grammar school programming, "**i** before **e** except after **c**." Some of you might have rummaged through a dictionary to find words like "leisure" and "seizure" and "seismic" with which to prove me wrong before telling me that you disagreed with my impression.

Those of us raised with the comforting certainty of, "**i** before **e** except after **c**" might feel the least little bit betrayed by the truth. I know that my eyebrows went up somewhat when someone paraded "leisure," "seizure" and "seismic" under my nose for the very first time. I felt as if a tiny, pristine part of a childhood fantasy had just become slightly tainted.

"I have the impression that you no longer love me. Tell me if you agree and correct me if you don't." If the other person says, "You have the correct impression, I no longer love you," you have obtained truth, albeit a painful one. As I said, prepare your Self to hear truths you may not like. It would seem healthier to know an unpleasant truth now, and to suffer with it for a short time while

An Ultimate Truth

you get over it, than to live in a lie for the rest of your life. Only you and you alone can properly evaluate the relative importance of those two options to your Self.

70
Six Seconds of Rolling Reality

Some scientists purportedly spent their grant money on a study to discover the length of "now."

They determined that 'now' lasted for only a few seconds: six I believe. I have no idea how the results came about or by what methodology the researchers arrived at their conclusions; but six seconds sounds about right. It probably takes about two seconds for our senses to fully register reality, another two seconds to integrate the new information with our past information and another two seconds to integrate it with our ongoing projections and anticipations of the immediate future.

For example, you suddenly see a rattlesnake in your path. All your senses register the snake. The first two seconds pass. You then compare your sense impressions with any past knowledge you might have in your memory under the heading of 'rattlesnake.' I could see that eating up another two seconds. Then, you add up your current sensory data and your past data about rattlesnakes and apply the total to your immediate future. Now you can use all this information to help you decide how to proceed.

Of course, If the rattlesnake in your path happens to measure about five feet in length **and** has fangs two inches long, dripping with deadly venom **and** has coiled itself ready to strike **and** has fixed its unblinking eyes upon you from a distance of about two feet while deafening you with the sound of its rattle, the entire process will probably take a lot less time than six seconds.

However, under normal conditions, six seconds still sounds about right. I correlate the 'six seconds of now' concept with the example I gave you earlier of the flashlight in a dark room representing our consciousness at work, focusing on only one lighted area at a time. We constantly integrate present sensory input with the memories of our past inputs and conclusions, then

An Ultimate Truth

we apply all of that to our future moments. Present, past and future; our reality of 'now' involves all three, all of the time. **I visualize it as sort of a 'rolling reality.'** The flashlight of our consciousness keeps rolling along registering and integrating, registering and integrating. The process continues during every waking moment of our existence. Even our dreams help us to integrate present realities with past realities, experiences and conclusions.

Visualize your moment of 'now' as a rolling reality in which you have your complete existence and your total consciousness or, as I have said before, your Self awareness.

Behind you stretches a past that no longer exists in your rolling reality, it only exists in your memory. Every real moment of 'now' creates a real memory of something that no longer exists. Some memories we retain, most we don't.

In front of you stretches a future that can only exist in your imagination as a fantasy projection of things to come. The word fantasy comes from a Greek word meaning "imagination."

Memories represent realities that no longer exist and imagination represents a future which does not yet exist. The reality of your 'now' rolls along with these two infinite unrealities in front and behind.

You only, actually, possess these few fleeting seconds of 'now.' If I yelled "**WOMBAT!**" at you this very instant, the word would only exist as you heard it. After my voice stopped, my loud word would only exist in the unreality of your memory, not in your reality of **that** moment.

If I said 'tomorrow' to you, your imagination would create all sorts of images about the day to come, each one of them uniquely yours. None of those images exist in reality yet, so we must define them as **un**realities. They only have life as fantasies and projections of your imagination.

If you look forward to anything, since it does not yet exist, you look forward to a fantasy, to an unreality. Once you experience

Six Seconds of Rolling Reality

the thing you anticipated, it immediately becomes a memory, another unreality.

Our rolling reality exists between the two unrealities of past and future: memory and imagination.

Everything you can ever have only truly exists in the moment you experience it. If you anticipate it, you create a fantasy which, as yet, has no reality. When you recall the memory, afterwards, you activate and engage in yet another unreality.

You only **have** this moment. The five words of the last sentence you just read now only exist in your memory, unless and until you reexperience them by reading them again.

Since you only have the moment of reality that you actually experience, **how** you experience that moment matters. It matters a lot. You will either experience it functionally or you will experience it dysfunctionally.

Your rolling reality needs a hub, a center, an axis, a fixed and stable place in the middle of constant change where you can build a level platform to stand on as you move along.

You will need that platform in order to view reality as it passes by the flashlight of your consciousness. You have to allocate some space, during every moment of your 'now,' for that viewing stand, so that you can watch the parade go by.

Freud would probably have labeled the viewing stand as the third major component of personality, the 'super ego' with its 'ego ideal' and its 'conscience.'

I prefer the term 'viewing stand.' Most people can comfortably conjure up an image of what one looks like. Only a few people really feel comfortable visualizing the concept of a 'super ego.'

We watch reality parade by us from the viewing stand. Everyone looks for exceptions at a parade. We look for the one person out of line in the ranks of the marching bands. We look for the one person to drop the baton they threw in the air. We look for

An Ultimate Truth

the one person passing by, waving to the crowds, who happens to look unhappy. We listen for a sour note in the music.

Businesses often manage by exception. Senior executives train middle managers to do their job without requiring much supervision. Then, the seniors will only have to deal with problems which exceed their managers' authority to resolve.

We must look for exceptions from the platform of our viewing stand. Exceptions to what? Exceptions to a functional physical, intellectual, emotional and spiritual reality.

We have to monitor reality from our platform and look for things that could hurt us. **We have to do this during some part of every moment of our rolling reality.**

Vigilance defines the process of monitoring reality during every moment of our existence and I will discuss it with you in the next chapter.

71

Vigilance

New Year's resolutions never work. Making decisions once a year, about anything, guarantees failure. Casting a searching, critical eye on our Selves only once every twelve months wastes energy and results in nothing.

The word 'monitoring' generally refers to a constant process, not an intermittent one. Checking up on your functionality once a week or once a month would have the same effect as breathing only once a week or once a month.

Vigilance means **constantly monitoring** your thoughts and emotions. It does not mean occasionally, it does not mean once in a while, it does not mean when you feel like it. Vigilance **must** become a full time part of you, a part of every moment of your rolling reality, **if** you intend to protect, develop and celebrate the rest of your life.

In case you find the idea of having to do something **all** the time objectionable, let me remind you that you already do something all the time. You make choices continually, remember? You choose to do, you chose not to do. You choose something or you choose nothing. You choose to choose or you choose not to choose. You choose to live or you choose to die.

You make many thousands of choices every day of your life. If you take your recovery seriously, you will choose to constantly monitor those choices to determine if they add value to your life or if they take value away. If you don't, you won't.

In an average day, you will make constructive choices and you will make destructive choices. You will make functional choices and you will make dysfunctional choices. If you don't monitor them, you won't ever discover the sources of your pain. You may know how to make changes but you won't know what to change.

An Ultimate Truth

As I said earlier, it makes no sense to expend all the energy necessary to build a brand new, functional house for your Self to live in and then not bother with any maintenance.

Pretty soon, your new house will crumble, leaving you with nothing but rubble. Even castles in the sky need regular dusting.

In the preceding chapters, I have addressed the process of recovering your functionality. If you follow what I have offered you and work as if your life depends on it, which it does, you will create 'high ground' for your Self in the middle of the swamp of dysfunction. You will have the knowledge, the power and the understanding you need to fight your way up to that high ground you have created. You will have the ability to stand up on it and feel the solid rock under your feet. You can raise your head, perhaps for the first time in your life, straighten your back and proclaim in a loud voice, "**I MATTER!**" You can feel the warmth of a sun you never thought existed. You can look around you and see the other people in the distance standing on the high ground that they too have earned. You will realize that your isolation has ended. You will feel your despair begin to fade. You may even smile and feel a desire to celebrate.

Without vigilance, I guarantee you won't smile or celebrate for long because the swamp of dysfunction will reclaim your high ground. It will send slime and corruption slithering over your footprints. Without vigilance, it won't take long for the muck and the mire to obliterate any trace of the high ground you once stood upon. And you, of course, will find yourself back in the ooze, up to your eyeballs in the same old pit. Only this time, you will suffer the extra agony of the memory of what you almost had and of those beautiful, priceless moments which you so briefly experienced. It will make the pain of your dysfunction worse than before you started recovery. You will experience all of your original pain **plus** the pain of knowing what you lost.

Vigilance requires you to monitor your situations, your beliefs and your emotions as well.

Vigilance

It requires you to ask the following questions: In what situation do I find myself? What beliefs do I have about this situation?

Never forget, your emotions will always reflect your **true beliefs**, not the ones you think you ought to hold, about any given situation.

Cultivate a constant awareness of your Self at the center of your rolling reality. Monitor your choices. Constantly ask your Self, "Constructive or destructive?" with regard to your choices. I always challenge clients to ask this question about every choice they make. Does a particular choice reflect your Self interest or your Self destruction?

Many regular cameras and video cameras have words or numbers that appear only to the eye of the viewer. They can show things like the date, the time, 'recording' or 'low battery.' I strongly recommend that you put three words on the window in your head through which you view **all** of reality. "Constructive or destructive?" A constant awareness of your answer to that question, regarding every choice you make, will help keep you out of trouble.

If you intend to hold on to your high ground, then you will have as your objective the maintenance of your position of strength during every moment of every day. Since goals define the measurable steps one takes to achieve an objective, your goals will consist of staying fully aware of every situation you find your Self in, monitoring your choices as to their constructive or destructive attributes and understanding what beliefs you bring to a situation. Job One, as you may remember, requires a created entity, you, me and everybody else, to protect, develop and celebrate the most important, most highly valued thing we know.

Vigilance means fighting to meet these goals. To the extent you accomplish them, you will meet your overall objective of sustaining your functionality.

An Ultimate Truth

Achieving functionality in the first place demands so much of us, it would seem a real tragedy to lose everything we worked for simply because we didn't feel like putting in the effort necessary to maintain it.

I pointed out to you earlier that we have all the power, all of the time. This means that at any given moment, we can use our personal power either to build or to destroy.

You can build a functional house for your Self to dwell in comfortably for the rest of your days and then destroy it through neglect. As in all things, you have the power to choose, **and you cannot avoid choosing something**.

You may value life. I hope you do. I do. Based on the proposition that you value life, I will further assume that you value your own life.

I have spent this entire book talking about the value of **your** life. I hope that as a result of our discussions, you will see your own life as the **most** valuable thing you know and have a greater ability to make constructive choices that will add value to that life.

However, not all people share your, our, view of the value of life. I have spent a lifetime attempting to understand the who, what, why, when, where and how of humanity. From the educated guesses about prehistoric humans, to the earliest evidence of those who actually left records, right up to the present, I have seen no evidence whatsoever that **groups** of people value life. You can read the same books and conduct the same research that I did and see it for your Self. Actually, history shows that, generally, the bigger the group, the less the people in that group value the life of an individual **outside** the group.

Religious holy books proudly describe the successful slaughter of legions as proof of a divine sanction. Inquisitions claim to kill in order to protect the purity of the faith. Wars enable nations to climb higher up the food chain as they come to value people's capacity to destroy more highly than their ability to build and create. When humans commit genocide and take each other's

Vigilance

lives by the thousands or by the millions, century after century, in culture after culture, it demonstrates a truth I don't like but that I must accept.

You have no guarantee that any other human will look at your life and consider it sacred. They might and they might not. History tells us that people in a group, whether religious, military, political, economic, cultural, social, ethnic, geographic or judicial, tend to devalue the life of an individual outside of **their** group.

The same person who values your life when they talk to you, eye to eye, may not value it at all when they see you through the eyes of their group.

So, my final observation regarding **your** choices wraps itself around what I have just said. Don't count on groups of other people to help you decide that your life has value. Historically, a group tends to look at an individual outside of the group as a disposable commodity, not as the most valuable thing **they** know.

The most valuable thing you know defines you. The most valuable thing I know, me, wishes the most valuable thing you know, you, safe passage through the swamps of dysfunction. Beware of the alligators, especially groups of them.

Thank you for walking with me. Thank you even more for letting me into your life.

The End

An Ultimate Truth

Epilogue

I want to tell you how proud I feel about what my husband, Geoffrey Hamilton, has done and continues to do. I think that helping others to get out of dysfunction deserves the status of the most important thing a person could do. I know its importance because I've been through it, personally. I never would have made it through alive without the kind of guidance Geoffrey has written about.

I can definitely use myself as an example of how far a person can come using the therapeutic process that this book describes. I did the inner work that you have just read about. I had to. It came down to doing it or dying. I made the choice to live. It looks like you may have made that choice as well. GOOD!! It may seem daunting, but the results will provide more than enough reward!

When I look back to what I did, and thought, and felt, before I did the work, I can barely recognize myself. I worked so hard at killing myself, letting others help to kill me and at hurting others. I never knew what my actions really accomplished or what drove me. I ran on a deadly auto-pilot. I **did** know that I didn't feel happy. I felt confused. It looked black inside my Self when I tried to look inside. Does this sound familiar to you?

Then I did the work. I cleaned myself out. (But that story could fill another book!) It took me about a year and a half. I worked **very** hard and earned my life back.

Now I have control of my life. I know what drives me, in any direction. I can control the negatives and enjoy the positives. I work hard at living life to the fullest (which really doesn't seem at all like work!) and I help others to do the same, when possible. When I look inside (which I do always) it looks bright and clear and feels safe and warm and wonderful.

An Ultimate Truth

I know that as you read through some parts of this book, you probably asked yourself something like "Why would I want to do all this work?" or else you thought, "This seems much too difficult!" Maybe you considered giving up on the process. I know because, at times, I thought that too. But don't. Don't give up. **This process works!** And, it rates as possibly the most important thing you'll ever do for yourself!

You may also think that, "An easier way must exist!" Well, yes and no. Mostly no. I can say, from experience, that you will find many, many other ways out of your discomfort. I can also say, from experience, that they don't **truly** work. They may distract us from our pain, numb us or overwhelm us, but they won't get us out of our dysfunction. They won't truly stop the pain. And, they won't always, permanently, work. We can't go around the pain, we have to go through it. It means more work, but much, much more gain.

Let me share with you some of the things that motivated me and kept me going. Maybe it will make some difference to you. I hope so.

A good friend of mine once asked a question of her class. It went something like this: "In the very deepest, innermost part of you, deep inside your soul, your heart, your mind, there exists a small kernel of joy. Why?" You may or may not have awareness of its existence but that small kernel of joy **does** dwell within you. Why do you think it even exists? During that class, many students proffered many different answers to her question. Her answer? "**It exists because you exist.**" The joy comes from a supreme happiness, a happiness just to exist! That touched me deeply and rang true with me.

If we want to know that feeling personally, to feel it as a constant, to nurture it, to spread it, then we must get out of our dysfunction. Dysfunction serves to limit, to decrease and even to preclude our ability to know this joy. I can vouch for that! Prior to working through my life-threatening dysfunction, that joy existed, inside of me, but it seemed such a long way off and hard to locate! Now I can feel it, every moment of my life; and it feels wonderful.

Epilogue

So much more than just pain and suffering exists inside of us. We have so much more that we can connect with: our joy, our inner child, our Selves, our Creator. **But**, to fully, permanently connect, we have to deal with our dysfunction first.

My powerful visualization of how dysfunction looked inside of me helped to motivate me. I would like to share it with you. Picture an infant, hardly able to crawl or a toddler, barely toddling. Picture a cold, stone wall all around the child, forming a small cell. Picture darkness without and within. Hear the small cries of the child. Picture too, a dark beast (mine looked like a rat), free to roam throughout any part of the large, dark expanse surrounding the cell. And, see a small chink in the wall of the stone cell. Every so often, a small hand comes out as if to reach for comfort; or an eye peeks out, waiting, waiting for someone to come. But the only answer: the threatening scuffle of the beast in the dark or the nip of sharp teeth. The child: you, your original Self. The wall: your dysfunction. The beast: your destructive beliefs and actions. The adult **you** wants to, needs to, hold that child **you**. The child **you** needs the adult **you** to save it. Please do. Every step out of dysfunction takes away one small stone from the cell, takes away a little power from the beast, shines a little light into the gloom inside. And, when you finish, you can hold that child and play with that child and become that child!

As I did the work, I increased my connection to my inner child, my Self, my joy, my high ground and my Creator. This helped me to go on, to go farther, to get out and stay out of dysfunction. Every step **out** of dysfunction has an accompanying step **into** connection.

My wish for you: to feel this moment of connection as you begin your inner work. It feels so beautiful and joyous! When you reach a difficult time and you feel you can't go on, recall your experience of connectedness. You had it at least once in your life, before dysfunction dragged you down. As you get into doing the work, you will add many more such precious moments to your reservoir of positive experiences. Draw from them. Let them give

An Ultimate Truth

you strength and inspiration to keep going. You will have definitely earned them.

Good luck in all your inner journeys!

Deborah Trevvett, loving wife of Geoffrey Hamilton

Index

A

1,2,3 pattern	100
Abuse, parental	47, 233
Abuse, mild or severe	238
Abuse, outrage about	237
Accepting reality as real	161
Accident	117
Accountability	234
Acknowledging abuse	238
Action beliefs	175-180
Actions: evidence of our beliefs	143
Affirmations: effect on beliefs	128
Anger, expressing	241
Anger: for survival	99-100
Anger, present vs. past	80
Anger, surfacing	246
Anger, writing about	242
Arguing	229
Attention getting	225
Attitude, definition of	66
Awareness, constant	269

B

Behavior, observing	146
Belief, power of	133
Belief system	123-126
Belief system, definition of	5
Beliefs determine actions	141
Beliefs: as an expression of your truth	124
Beliefs: below consciousness	168
Beliefs, identifying old	175
Beliefs: in fantasies	125
Beliefs: of a newborn	124-125
Beliefs, realistic or unrealistic	152
Beliefs, true	269
Beliefs, unknown	172
Beliefs, your list of	150
Below conscious mind	167-169
Below consciousness, preprogrammed	134
Black and white emotional states	110, 217
Blame	233
Body language	222
Brain: how it works	167-169
Bubble, living in	225
Bulletproof and immortal	111

C

Changing beliefs	211-215
Chaos	77-78
Choices: no mistakes	53-55
Choosing to do the work, or not	177

Codependency 69
Codependency: external vs. internal focus 41-42
Cognitive dissonance 189
Communications 221-224
Comparison 139
Compass of emotions, 4 points of 98
Confronting parents 238
Consciousness: as a flashlight 167
Constructive or destructive 269
Constructive vs. destructive 33-34
Convictions, old beliefs become 128
Cope, Circumstances and Change 249
Core beliefs 5, 123, 177
Core beliefs, dysfunctional 181-185
Core beliefs, changing 211-215
Core beliefs, when we evaluate them 205
Crisis 206

D

Death 26-27
Default 117
Degrees of achievement 195
Denial of reality 59-61
Disagreement 229

Distraction 84-85
Distress, psychological 157
Divorcing: from parents 236
Dreams 247-248
Dreams, recurring 247
Dysfunction: general 121, 188
Dysfunction: crisis turning point 29-30
Dysfunction, discussion of 11

E

Emotional dysfunction, causes of 151
Emotions, steps preceding 153-155
Emotional healing 107
Emotional payoff, desire for 133
Emotional radar 147
Emotions 97-98, 101
Emotions: in dreams 247-248
Emotions: primary or secondary 151
Empathy 227
Eustress 157
Evaluation: defined 139
Exceptions, perceiving 266
Existence and consciousness 26-27
Experience, consciousness illuminates 167

Index

F

Facts and feelings	260
Family system	43
Fantasies, dreams and magic, screens of	166
Fantasy	126
Fantasy vs. reality	125-126
Fear: as a motivator	56
Fear: relationship to anger	112
Fear: to help survive	111-112
Fear: unhealthy	112
Floors: of the brain	167
Forgive and forget	238
Forgiveness	233-239
Free will	119

G

Gene pool	134
Genes	134-135
Genetic coding	134-135
Goals and objectives	269
Grief: for survival	105-107
Grieving lost moments	166
Groups, dangers of	270
Guilt: controlling with	43-47
Guilt: earned and unearned	255

H

Heredity	134
Hidden beliefs, identifying	173-174
High ground	268
High ground: safe haven	101-103
Highs: relationships and addictions	91-92
Hope	159
Hundred strangers	145

I

Imagination	264
Information, transfer of	221
Intellectual dysfunction, definition of	120
Intellectual dysfunction: resulting from fantasy	126
Intuition	117

J

Joy: for survival	109-110

K

Killer words	158, 187

L

Language, development of	143
Life: gift or curse	31-32
Life: the most important thing	129-131
Living: on purpose or accidentally	119-120
Loss	105-107
Love	197

Love of Self	35-39
Love, acquiring definition of	198-203
Love, expression of	201
Love, in	202
Loving acts	198-199
Loving the Self	200

M

Mattress, beating	243
Megalomania	153
Memories	264
Mind: like a dry sponge	144
Mixed emotions	163
Moment, this	263
Monitoring	266
Mood altering	91
More-than-half	224
Most significant core belief	6, 129
Mystery: comfortable or uncomfortable	21-27
Mystical shortcuts	118
Mysticism, characteristics of	15-18

N

Natural market	253
Nature/nurture	134
Never 'good enough'	193
New tapes, making	214-215
No guard at the gate	171
Now, length of	263

O

Obsessive/compulsive vs. addiction	84-85
Opinions	229
Opinions into beliefs	127
Options, Choices and Consequences	53-61
Overeating	161

P

Pain points	209
Pain vs. no-pain	210
PAL (Permit, Allow, Let)	102
Parental duties	234
Parenting	234-238
Parents, as interpreters	193
Pencils, breaking	243
People pleaser	251
Perfection	191-196
Personal power, loss of	55-56
Pillows, bashing	243
Plato	191
Power	71-74
Power: constructive	72
Power: destructive	73-74
Powerless vs. powerful	71-74
Procrastination vs. deferral	75-76
Professional philosophers	208

Index

Q

Questions, rhetorical	259
Questions, survival	145

R

Reacting: to beliefs	137
Reactive behavior	225
Reality, rolling	263
Reason	113-115
Reason: an option?	118
Recovery, stages of	29
Relationship beliefs	127
Relationships: destructive	92
Relationships: healthy	88
Relationships: with others	87-89
Relationships: with Self	87
Religion vs. theology vs. spirituality	9-10
Repressed emotions, tuning in to parents'	147
Repression	79-85
Repression: of anger	93-94
Repression: of sadness	106-107
Repression vs. suppression	80
Responsibilities: to protect, develop and celebrate	8
Responsibility	53, 63, 64
Retirement	207
Revelation	117
Revenge	235-237

S

Sadness: for survival	105
Scripts, roles developing	145
Seeing reality	161
Seesaw model	64, 109
Self esteem	35
Self interest	49-52
Selfishness	35-52
Self, aspects of	11-12
Self, separation from	82
Sequence of beliefs acquisition	127-128
Shame	45
Sharing	88
Situations: defined	162
Situations, beliefs regarding	175-176
Situations, percentages of	162-165
Speaking in public	176
Spiritual: excuses	19
Spiritual: isolation and separation	103
Spirituality, definition of	7
Stress	157-159
Stress: positive or negative, depending on belief system	123
Styles, coping	249
Successes and failures, taking responsibility for	63-64
Suffering: as a choice	67-69

An Ultimate Truth

Summary: first half of book 121
Survival: as a newborn 44-47
Survival: during childhood 43
Survival tools 97, 113
Sympathy 227
Systems, educational 135

T

Therapeutic relationship,
the value of 65-66
Therefore 178
Thought patterns: dysfunctional 217-219
Time: treating with respect 260
Trap door 171
Trophy polishing 67-69
Truth, telling the 260
Turning point 29

U

Ultimate truth: answered 21
Ultimate truth: revisited 13
Ultimate truths, statements of 2
Universal agreement, search for 1
Unpardonable act 235

V

Vegetative state 158
Victim, voluntary 255
Victimization, by others 71
Viewing stand 265
Vigilance 227, 267-271
Violent relationships 201

W

Walls, raising the height of 193
Win-win 225-226

Ordering Information

To obtain a copy of this book, please send check or money order for **$26.95 per book** ($21.95 plus $5.00 S&H) to:

>NORTHWOODS CONSULTING
>6107 S.W Murray Blvd,. Suite 351
>Beaverton, Oregon 97008-4467
>
>Please allow 4-6 weeks for delivery.